CREATING COMMUNITY

CREATING COMMUNITY

The Jews of Springfield, Missouri

Mara W. Cohen Ioannides

Greene County Historical Society Press

Springfield, Missouri

DEDICATION

*For those who came before
and those yet to come.*

Contents

Acknowledgments

There are numerous people I must thank for helping along the way. The many families, archives, museums, and synagogues who provided images for this book. They definitely make it a more relatable and interesting text. Joan Porter-Hampton, curator of The History Museum on the Square, and Jami Lewis, former archivist at The History Museum on the Square, and Lindsey Young, former archivist at The History Museum on the Square, have all been irreplaceable resources. David Richards, former Head of Special Collections at Meyer Library, Missouri State University, who made the Ozarks Jewish Archive (OJA) a reality. Anne Marie Baker, current Head of Special Collections, and the staff there for making the OJA possible and accessible and the assistance they offered. My colleagues and friends at the Midwest and Western Jewish Studies Associations for their support and ideas as I worked through this project. The community at Temple Israel, Springfield, Missouri for their support and interest in this project. The Board of the Greene County Historical Society for agreeing to publish this book. Angie Piercy and Anne Marie Baker for editing drafts must be thanked. Finally, my husband Rob and daughter Sasha who now know more about the Jews of Springfield than they ever wanted to because they listened politely to me as I made my discoveries.

Introduction

The purpose of this book is multifold. Firstly, there is no history of the Jews of Springfield and because they played, and still do, an important role in the city's history there should be one. Secondly, only during this century has the study of small Jewish communities (those under 500 people), of which Springfield is one, really come in to its own, especially with the publication by Lee Shai Weissbach of *Jewish Life in Small-Town America: A History* in 2005. There is also a resurgence in Midwestern Studies and this book should help fill the lacuna of ethnic studies within the field. Finally, the Jewish community has commented on the need for its history to be recorded since the latter half of the last century.

Locals' desire to remember and understand Springfield's history is attested to by the recent move, expansion, and renaming of the local history museum and the amazing turn-out they get at their events. Additionally, there is a Facebook page devoted to Springfield, Missouri history that has over 2,500 members who share photographs and memories.

Scholars have come to understand that despite the huge populations of Jews in urban areas, the majority of Jews actually live scattered across the country in small communities and their experiences are just as valid as those in large communities. Weissbach is quite critical of accounts that do not contextualize histories of small communities. It is my hope this book helps to historically situate Springfield's Jewish community within the context of Missouri and United States History, while elaborating on the broader American Jewish experience.

Beginning in 1977, Rabbi David Wucher, at the time the rabbi in Springfield, suggested that the Temple Israel Board of Directors create a museum "because not many people are informed about the local [Jewish] history."[1] In 1987, Prof. Ken Betsalel, a congregation member, offered to do an oral history project for the congregation.

The following year, probably on the behest of Betsalel, the congregation turned to the Union of American Hebrew Congregations for assistance in creating a display of their history. Then in 1989, Cheryl Bluestein, a congregation member, requested that she be given the oral history project so that she could use it as part of her doctoral research. Finally, in the 1990s, Prof. Marc Cooper, a former president of the congregation and professor of history at Missouri State University, received a Missouri Humanities Council grant to conduct an oral history project of the Jewish community. With the help of student Julie Henigan, they gathered interviews with the oldest members of the community and have since donated them to the Ozarks Jewish Archive (OJA) in Special Collections and Archives, Meyer Library, Missouri State University.

The OJA opened in April of 2004. It began with materials collected as part of the Telling Traditions project. This project, co-directed by myself and Dr. Rachel Gholson, followed the life of Temple Israel for a full year and included video, photograph, and audio recordings. With additions from families and the congregation, the collection grows regularly. It was not until the beginning of the new century that I was able to get a display of all the available Religious School and confirmation photographs, full-time rabbis, and places of worship hung on the synagogue walls and create an exhibition of religious items for our guests. Because most of the congregation are new to the community and the history has not been well-publicized, this has created a positive vibe in the congregation and more respect among the non-Jewish community.

The purpose of this book, therefore, is both to reach out to the locals, Jews and non-Jews, to give them a better understanding of their community, as well as to provide scholars and other researchers with a new expanded understanding of the Ozarks. It is certainly not complete. That is not the intent. The intent of this publication is to show how the Jewish community of Springfield, Missouri came to be, how it has integrated into the larger community, and how it represents a facet of Jewish experience in the United States.

CHAPTER I

American Jewish History and Missouri History

First Jews in America

In THE FALL OF 1654, THE *St. Catrina* arrived in the port of New Amsterdam, now New York City. It carried 23 Jews from former Dutch protectorate of Recife in Brazil. Having previously escaped persecution in Spain, the refugees were again forced to flee by the Portuguese Inquisition in the aftermath of the reconquest of Recife. Co-religionists Jacob Barsimon and Solomon Pietersen had already taken up in residence in the New Amsterdam a few months earlier, although there is some debate as to whether the twenty-three arrived first. After the *St. Catrina*, later in 1654 or maybe early 1655, another group of Jews, this time from Amsterdam, landed in the colony on the *Peereboom*. These were the first Jews to settle in what was to become the United States of America.

Some of the Jewish immigrants who arrived on the *Peereboom* had significant ties to the Dutch West India Company. Descendants of Asser Levy speculate that he went to New Amsterdam because of the trading opportunities arising between Amsterdam and New Amsterdam. Levy discovered, however, that the acceptance of Jews he had experienced in Holland was not duplicated in its North American colony.

In Dutch Brazil, Jews were recognized as full citizens of Holland—a privilege not accorded to Jews who lived in other Dutch provinces. In 1629, the Dutch had granted freedom of religion to the Jews and Catholics, allowing them to practice their faiths publicly; something not permitted in northern Europe. This was given to the Jews, not because they were liked as a religious group, but because they were needed to continue the international trade. While Jews could not work in the traditional areas of trade in Holland, they monopolized trade with Portugal and its colonies because of the Sephardic (Jews of Spanish descent) Crypto (Jews who pretended to be Catholic) ties already in place. This must have been a significant factor in

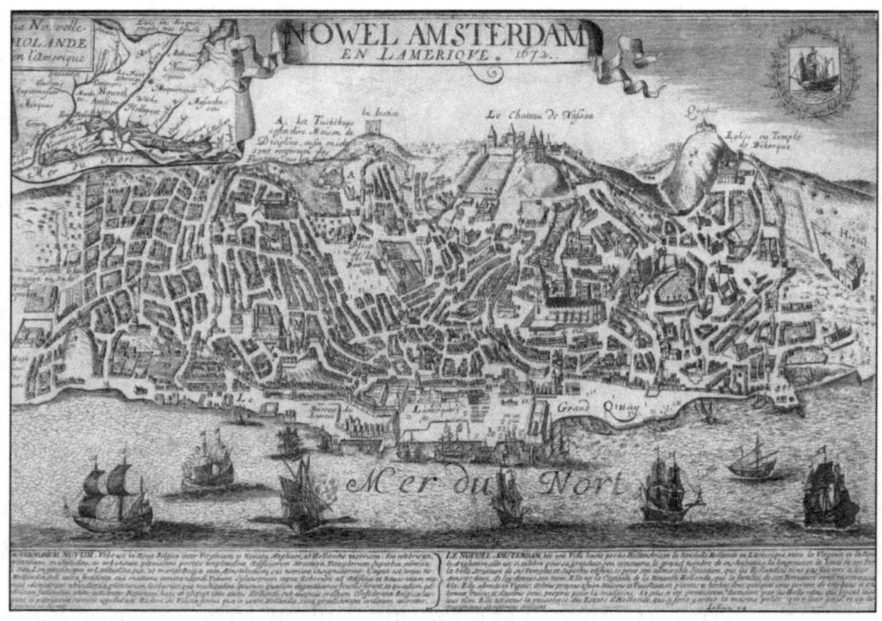

New Amsterdam, New Orange, by Picryl, 1650

the Jews' reactions to their situation in New Amsterdam where antisemitism stifled their rights as Dutch citizens.

Governor Peter Stuyvesant tolerated the Jews who arrived from Amsterdam, including Barsimon, Levy, and Pietersen, because they had money and connections. However, he strongly objected to the Brazilian Jews because they were, in his eyes, "such hateful enemies and blasphemers of the name of Christ" being "allowed . . . to infect and trouble this new colony."[1] The real concern for Stuyvesant was that the Brazilian refugees were indigent, having arrived at the colony deeply in debt to the shipping company. Moreover, because the Jewish population was so small, it fell to the broader community had to support the immigrants, in conflict with Dutch laws requiring Jews to support their own. Nevertheless, two more ships carrying Jews arrived in 1654 and 1655, not only enlarging the population of New Amsterdam, but also expanding the Jewish population of the city.

In March 1656, five Jewish men, who had been solid contributors to the civic life of New Amsterdam for nearly two years, petitioned the advisory council to become burghers, or citizens. In the Netherlands, not all city residents were burghers. Jews could only become burghers by buying the right and proving they were productive merchants. Abraham de Lucena, Jacob Cohen Henricques, Salvador Dandrada, Joseph d'Acosta, and David Fiera offered the council 500 flourins, and pledged "to contribute according to their means" to the city's upkeep.[2] The council consisting of Stuyvesant, Nicasius DeSille, and Jan LaMontagne refused the request and suggested "the broad question be once again put to the lords directors [of the Honorable West

Governor Peter Stuyvesant
From: Benson J. Lossing, *The Pictorial Field-Book of the Revolution*,
Harper & Bros., 1852, p. 783.

India Company of the United Provinces of the Netherlands]."[3] Unbeknownst to the council, in Holland on March 13, 1656, the directors had dispatched a letter giving "consent . . . to the Jews to go to New Netherland and there to enjoy the same . . . civil and political liberties"[4] they were granted in the metropole. Dandrada, Henricques, DeLucena, and d'Acosta resubmitted their petition to the council the following year, after being made aware of the contents of the March 13, 1656 letter. With the directors having already reprimanded Stuyvesant the previous summer for not following their rules, the four petitioners reminded the council "that our Nation enjoys in the City of Amsterdam in Holland the Burgher right."[5] That d'Acosta was a principal shareholder in the Dutch West India Company certainly encouraged the reprimand and the eventual recognition that the Jewish petitioners' received as burghers. What had been evident to the Jews in New Amsterdam, must have become plain to the directors as well. There was more than acceptable levels of antisemitism in the New Amsterdam government, since the laws of the Netherlands were regularly being ignored.

Less than a decade after the Jews had been conferred burgherhood, New Amsterdam passed to English control to become New York City in 1664. The Jewish community found its former freedoms greatly constricted under English rule as they would have to wait until 1740 to be granted citizenship by the Parliament, even as the New York General Assembly had passed numerous special acts naturalizing Jews on strictly individualized bases. The usual oath required of those taking on the mantel was changed for those "person[s] professing the Jewish Religion" so that they did not have to say "videlict" meaning "upon the true Faith of a Christian."[6] Fought for by Jews in England and clearly supported by the Jews in New York City who were accustomed to having a certain level of political power, this changed the scope of what is a citizen of a country. Jews and Gentiles considered Jews to be full citizens because ten Jews, ten Jewish citizens, signed the Address of the Citizens of Philadelphia and of the Liberties thereof to President Washington in 1783. One of these ten was Haym Salomon who practically bankrolled the Revolution.

Elsewhere in the English North American colonies, the freedoms that the Dutch had extended to Jews in New Amsterdam in 1656 were emulated in Charles Town in 1669, as the Fundamental Constitutions of Carolina, written by John Locke, included:

> Jews, heathens, and other dissenters from the purity of the
> christian [*sic*] religion, may not be scared and kept at a distance
> from it, but by having an opportunity of acquainting themselves
> with the truth and reasonableness of its doctrines, and the
> peaceableness and inoffensiveness of its professors, may by good
> usage and persuasion, and all those convincing methods of
> gentleness and meekness, suitable to the rules and design of the
> gospel, be won over to embrace and unfeignedly receive the truth;
> therefore any seven or more persons, agreeing in any religion,
> shall constitute a church or profession, to which they shall give
> some name, to distinguish it from others.[7]

Reflecting Locke's commitment to religious tolerance, Carolina's constitution even went so far as to outlaw antisemitism, insisting that "no man shall use any reproachful, reviling, or abusive language, against any religion of any church or profession."[8]

Perhaps the most powerful advocacy on behalf of recognizing Jews as full citizens of the United States can be found in President Washington's response to the letter from Levi Sheftal. In his letter, the president of the Hebrew-Congregation of Savannah congratulated Washington on his election in 1789. Washington told the congregation: "I rejoice that a spirit of liberality and philanthropy is much more prevalent than it formerly was among the enlightened nations of the earth; and that your brethren will benefit thereby in proportion as it shall become still more extensive."[9] Washington's response to Moses Sexias and the Hebrew Congregation in Newport was even more strongly worded, as he not only referred his Jewish correspondents as citizens but hopes they will continue to "enjoy the good will of the other inhabitants" of the United States.[10] Finally, in his letter to the congregations in Philadelphia, New York, Charleston, and Richmond, Washington again identifies the Jews as "fellow citizens."[11] When the "Father of His Country" called Jews citizens, there should have been no further doubt that they were.

The Jewish community in the United States continued to grow with an influx of Western European Jews from Holland, France, Germany, and England, eventually reaching an estimated three thousand in 1818 and doubling in nearly a decade to six thousand in 1826. By 1840, when Springfield was incorporated, the beginning of mass immigration by Germans—both Christian and Jewish—had brought the population to approx imately 15,000. Jews remained a tiny minority in the United States, as they represented only 0.1 percent during the 1800s. Indeed there were, in 1870, only 161 towns in the United States with more than one hundred Jews. They were, nonetheless, central to the American story.

Missouri's Early History

The region now known as the State of Missouri was inhabited by Paleoindians as early as 9250 BCE. When the first Europeans arrived in the area, they were met by the Osage and Kansa. What would later be named the Ozarks, where the town of Springfield would be built, was occupied by the Osage, Caddos, and Quapaw.

The Jacob Philipson House in Ste. Genevieve. *Courtesy the author.*

The Spaniard Hernando de Soto and his team were the first Europeans to visit Missouri in 1541. De Soto and his men were violent plunderers and devastated the natives with smallpox and cholera. It was not until 1673 that Louis Joliet, Jacques Marquette, and five others left Michigan and headed south exploring the Mississippi and Arkansas Rivers. When René-Robert Cavelier continued this exploration in 1682, he claimed the region for France, since there were no Spanish settlements. The first French settlers were farmers and traders, specializing in manufactured goods and alcohol that they would trade for fur and slaves.

Americans in French Territory

The French and Indian War (1754-1763) changed the European ownership of the region. The treaty to end the war resulted in the region, called Louisiana, being turned over to the Spanish. The French headquarters moved to St. Louis in 1765 and turned the relatively uninhabited region into the center of the French kingdom in North America, although they were under Spanish rule.

The American Revolution spurred westward expansion. A group of Virginia militia lead by George Rogers Clark captured Cahokia, a community just east of St. Louis on the eastern side of the Mississippi. However, the British Lt. Gov. Patrick Sinclair retaliated, using Native Americans as troops. The Spanish defended their territory and won. The east side of the Mississippi was under the control of the fledgling United States. To solidify their hold on their territory, in 1784 the Spanish insisted that any non-Spaniard who wished to live or trade in the region had to swear an oath of loyalty to Spain and Catholicism.

With a rapidly growing population, some believed that the United States needed to expand to the West. In 1803, Spain ceded the Louisiana territory to France and less than a month later the French sold the territory to the United States. For $15 million, President Thomas Jefferson bought 827,987 square miles of land. By 1803, many Americans already had slipped across the border and begun to stake claims in the Louisiana. Indeed, as far back as 1789, Col. George Morgan, who worked for the Spanish governor, had established a settlement at New Madrid, attracting American immigration into the territory. Moreover, Americans were not the only groups attracted to the region, as it was during this period that the Kickapoo tribe relocated from Illinois to the Ozarks, where they built a town in the area of what would become Springfield.

Jews in Missouri

An 1803 census of New Madrid, included a listing of Ezekial Block, who is labeled "a German Jew." His family became influential in St. Louis. Among the early American immigrants to St. Louis were Joseph, Jacob, and Simon Philipson. The three Polish-born brothers first lived in Philadelphia, but they had "business ventures into the Missouri Territories."[11] Joseph settled in St. Louis on December 13, 1807 and became the first American merchant to establish a permanent store in St. Louis. He was one of the initial investors in the Missouri Bank in 1817 and probably opened the first distillery west of the Mississippi. Jacob arrived in 1808, and, in 1811, moved south to Ste. Genevieve where he continued as a merchant for a few years. However, after he married, he returned to St. Louis where he taught English, French, and German. The last brother to arrive was Simon who joined Joseph in the brewing business in 1821.

It was in St. Louis that the first synagogue west of the Mississippi was established. Though the community had already been worshipping together

An 1840 view Front Street in St. Louis where the first Jewish congregation west of the Mississippi is presumed to have worshipped. by John Casper Wild
Courtesy Missouri History Museum.

for four years, in 1841, it adopted a constitution and chose the name United Hebrew Congregation, becoming just the twentieth synagogue in the United States.

The earliest demographic data we have for the state of Missouri is 1870, when there was estimated a Jewish population of 7,385 in the state out of the suggested 229,087 Jews in the entire nation. At this point, *The American Jewish Year Book* lists Jewish communities in Missouri sizable enough to merit its attention in St. Louis, St. Joseph, and Kansas City. Only three years later, there were 35,000 Jews in Missouri and 778,107 Jews in the entire country. The rapid population increase was caused by the exodus of Jews from Czarist Russia as the antisemitism there became dangerous. The story of Jews in Springfield, Missouri begins in the 1860s during the Civil War.

Founding of Springfield

Even as late as 1804, there was no permanent European settlement in the Ozarks, as French and Spanish colonization had focused on securing settlements and trading post along the Mississippi River. American colonization of the Trans-Mississippi accelerated after the War of 1812. Henry Schoolcraft stopped east of what would become Springfield during his

1818-1819 adventure and described the landscape in *Journal of a Tour into the Interior of Missouri and Arkansaw*: "[the] country [is] characterized by gentle sloping hills, well wooded with oak and hickory, with some extensive prairies, and a pretty fertile black soil . . . on the banks of [the] James River . . . are found extensive bodies of the choicest land, covered by a large growth of forest-trees and cane, and interspersed with prairies, oak, maple, white and black walnut, elm, mulberry, hackberry, and sycamore, are the common tress and attain a very large size. On the west commences a prairie of unexplored extent...covered with tall rank grass."[12]

The Louisiana Territory was in truth under the control of Native Americans, and some Euro-Americans had considered the region as a potential outlet for Indian removal. The American appetite for land, however, proved insatiable.

John P. Pettijohn, a Revolutionary War soldier, left Ohio in 1818 with 24 members of his immediate and extended family to make a new home in the Missouri Territory, settling in the Ozarks. On March 6, 1820, Missouri entered the union of states as a slave state. By 1821, a smaller group of Pettijohn's family had erected a cabin eight miles from what is now Springfield. In the fall of 1829, Madison and J. P. Campbell, who were members of the Pettijohn clan, left Tennessee and stopped eight miles from what is now Springfield. They marked their claim and began construction of their new home.

Territorial govenor William Clark, however, had assigned the area to the Delaware after the Treaty of St. Mary's had ceded lands in Indiana. Settlers of European descent were required to leave. The federal government intervened on behalf of American settlers in 1830, when it moved the Delaware to a "permanent" reservation in Kansas, allowing Pettijohn and one of his sons to return to their cabin. In the spring of 1830, A. J. Burnett became the first person of European descent to build on what was to become Springfield. Shortly thereafter, there was a grocery and stockyard in the future town. At this time, the population of the state of Missouri was 66,586 and the population of the county, then called Wayne, was 1,614.

The following year Joseph Rountree became the area's first schoolteacher at a subscription school in a chimneyless, doorless, dirt-floored cabin. It "was a one-room frame house" and "the road to [the] school was through a forest of oak and other hardwood trees," as William Rountree remembered.[13] The community was organized into lots in 1835, which included a public square. There were two blacksmiths, a cabinet maker, a hotel, and three stores. Before it was even incorporated in 1838, the community participated in the 1836 presidential election. Local lore says the name comes from "the *spring* . . . under the hill, and the *field* on the hill," although one of the founders of the community requested the town be named for his former town of Springfield, Tennessee.[14]

The first phase of settlement of what has been called the Old Ozarks Frontier, had been initiated by the French Creole after the sale Louisiana to the United States. These migrants were soon followed by Appalachian transplants. This group was of Scotch-Irish descent. Since these folk were of British origin, historian Brooks Blevins explains, "the region's pioneer settlers [before the Civil War] possessed a homogeneity rarely witnessed west of the Mississippi."[15] They were used to a more isolated life and settled into the hill country. While they had southern tendencies, they preferred to be considered Ozarkers over Missourians. Thus, until 1840, the Ozarks remained sparsely populated, as most of the region had no more than eighteen people per square mile, although statewide the population had increased more than five-fold to 383,702. Meanwhile, Wayne County had been renamed Greene and had a population of 6,552, while 344 residents could be counted in the town of Springfield.

The first bank, a State Bank of Missouri, opened in 1845, making the town more than a trading center. The first high school, Southwest Missouri High School, opened in 1850. The telegraph arrived in 1860 connecting Springfield to Jefferson City, the state capitol, just after the first stagecoach and overland mail delivery in 1858. As the community grew, they realized that they had to make improvements to the town infrastructure. In 1859, the city council had the streets and sidewalks around the town square improved and began work on a new county courthouse and jail. These upgrades were designed to make the town more appealing to new settlers and businesses.

The strongest desire of the people in the community was for a railroad to connect them to rest of the state and, thus, the country. Beginning in 1841, Springfield and Greene County residents held rallies to get support for a railroad. The county eventually purchased stock in what was to become the road for the rail. By the 1860s, the railroad made it easier for stock to arrive in the city, even if it had not quite reached Springfield. Once the railroad finally arrived in 1870, Springfield swelled as it became the fifth most populous in the state by 1900. Moreover, the railroad transformed Springfield into Missouri's fourth largest manufacturing center and its largest union city.

The charge of the First Iowa Regiment with General Lyon at it's head, at the Battle of Wilson's Creek August 10, 1861. *Courtesy of The Library of Congress.*

Civil War

Missouri, as a border state, during the Civil War was full of contention. The state considered leaving the Union, but never did act on this idea. In reality, the state was largely filled with Union sympathizers. Though Springfield was one of the towns in the region that had a sizable slave population, secession in Greene County could draw only on a very vocal minority for support.

Though much of the combat in the Trans-Mississippi was characterized by guerilla warfare by irregular units, Greene County was the site of major engagements at Springfield in October 1861, and, again, in January 1863. Ten miles away at the battle of Wilson's Creek on August 10, 1861, Brig. Gen. Nathaniel Lyon fell while leading the 2nd Kansas Infantry in an attack on Confederate positions on "Bloody Hill." The battle witnessed the highest percentage of deaths among Union soldiers in any battle during the war.

However, it was the anti-guerrilla policy that Union forces enacted with General Order No. 11 that had the most lasting effect on the Missouri. The measures devastated the state, as they were effectively a rehearsal for the total warfare General William Tecumseh Sherman later prosecuted in his

Savannah Campaign in 1864. Divided loyalties had set neighbor against neighbor, while the Confederate and Union armies burned farms and bridges to punish partisans and deny their enemies resources. Those farms spared the destruction were otherwise allowed to lay fallow. The rail lines not destroyed by the scorched earth policies were not maintained. The war slowed the development of rail in the Ozarks, as lines were not extended into the center of southwestern Missouri until well after the end of the conflict. Therefore, the trip to Rolla, 120 miles away was "over a rough, rocky wagon road, up and down hill, over the rolling hills of the Ozarks," as Joseph Rountree described it.[16] Nevertheless, land in the state was inexpensive and economic opportunities were abundant, attracting a growing immigrant population. This is dubbed the second phase, or New South phase, of Ozarks history.

While the size of the community changed little after the Civil War, the demographics changed dramatically. The local slave holders had fled south with their slaves during the war. Meanwhile, many soldiers who had remained in the region after the war and sent for their families, if they had any. This altered Springfield in some significant ways, as a large number of laborers, whose political leanings reflected more northern sensibilities, were now available to work.

Antisemitism

From the end of the Civil War to the early 1880s, Germans, both Christian and Jewish, were the largest portion of the immigrants to the United States. German immigrants came to the Ozarks prior to the war. They lived in the areas on the Missouri and Mississippi Rivers. Towns, such as Dutchtown and Hermann, had been founded in the 1830s. But in the post-war era, economic uncertainty in Germany sparked an influx of German immigrants to the United States. Railroad executives actively recruited Germans to work on the railroad, urging the people of Springfield to set aside nativist sentiment and to welcome the new arrivals as citizens. Springfield saw its largest German immigration during Reconstruction, and presumably there was great deal of social cohesion among Christian and Jewish Germans given their shared language and cultural traits, as well as the relatively small size of the town. Antisemitism in small towns, which Springfield was until the turn of the twentieth century, was "muted." Because of the intimacy of relationships in a small-town environment, it was hard for antisemites to maintain their distrust of the imagined "other."

A 1924 Ku Klux Klan meeting in what is now known as Fantastic Caverns.
Courtesy History Museum on the Square.

It should be noted, however, that what is considered antisemitic now is certainly not what was considered so in the nineteenth century.

The Jews were less than 1 percent of the local population. Thus, notoriously insular Ozarkers might find these people with different beliefs problematic. Not all Christians in the area were aware there was supposed to be a Jewish "problem." Lyle Owen, retired professor at Carnegie Institute of Technology (now Carnegie Mellon University), lived in Coon Creek outside of Branson, and attended what is now Missouri State University in Springfield. According to Owen, he "never thought" about there being Jews on campus, and "it never occurred to me to blame a whole people for the work of a small group of power-entrenched and sect-blinded ancient priests."[17] It would take the rise of the second Ku Klux Klan (KKK) to sound the alarm about the danger of foreign influence in the 1920s and 1930s.

From the perspective of Hiram W. Evans, the third Imperial Wizard of the Klan, the place of the American Jew was "that of the middle-man."[18] So long as the Jews remained in their separate place and did not intermarry, the KKK had no serious problem with them. Brooks Blevins notes that "the Klan's prominence in . . . north central Arkansas counties, such as Searcy and Boone, indicate the organization's influence in the Ozarks."[19]

They engaged in vigilante justice throughout the Arkansas Ozarks, and one could presume in the Missouri Ozarks, as well. After all, as Blevins emphasizes, the KKK "represented the social and political concerns of the mainstream, not those of a displaced, backward, peripheral group."[20] Their focus was the African American community. As historian Charles C. Alexander explains, "there is little evidence of overt antipathy on the part of the Klan towards Jews in Texas, Arkansas, Louisiana, or Oklahoma" from which we can conclude that the Missouri Ozarks Klan had much the same feelings.[21]

The Springfield Klan in the 1920s was focused on moral issues and anti-union activities, so that they invited a Jew to join. They believed unions to be socialist and, thus, anti-Christian. This Klansman clearly did not understand the 1916 Klan constitution that included the statement in Article II: "the objects of this Order shall be to unite white male persons, native born Gentile citizens of the United States" or the Klansman's Creed that emphasizes "the tenets of the Christian religion."[21] Nor did he appear to fully recognize that the "Principles and Purposes of the Knights of the Ku Klux Klan" explained "Klansmen are not 'against' the Catholics or 'against' the Jews, but are 'for' Protestant Christianity."[22] During this relatively early period the local KKK was more concerned with community morals, than racism or nativism, especially in Arkansas and Oklahoma, and so one could presume in the Missouri Ozarks as well.

Considering the minority status of Jews in the Ozarks, where they represented barely 2 percent of the population, the Klan's relative inattention to the local community was understandable, as the organization was far more concerned with larger Jewish population centers in the East. Moreover, the Jewish experience in Springfield was consistent with larger patterns observed throughout the United States. Small-town antisemitism tended to be subtle, as its practitioners were often conflicted in their bigotry. In cities, there were typically large numbers of Jews who were able to maintain distance from the antisemite's community, but, in small towns, Jews were hard to avoid. During the 1910s, Bill Karchmer, son of the scrap metal dealer Ben Karchmer, did not believe there was antisemitism. He contends that what little anti-Jewish sentiment there was was the expression of jealousy that the majority of the store owners were Jewish by their non-Jewish competitors. Other local Jews concur with Karchmer's assessment that there was little overt antisemitism. Jews who grew up in Springfield believed that their cultural identity was almost never made an issue. There were unsettling moments at Christmas time and the occasional expression of outrage over the killing of Jesus leveled at the lone Jewish student by a Christian student, but most interactions were amicable.

While the public schools included Christian themes, the school administration and teachers often did not understand the implications of their actions. Some of the Jewish students did not either. In the 1930s, the junior high put on Christmas productions about Jesus and the Jewish students had no problem participating in them.

There was a small group of Springfieldians who believed that Jews were the reason the United States had entered World War II. The controversy became contentious when it was allowed to spill over onto the playground. Jewish parents were made aware of the situation and once the matter was brought the attention of the school officials, the insensitivity and disrespect was put to a stop.

In the early 1960s, Simone Lotven brought home the school handbook which included an expectation "that students would behave as good Christians."[24] Her mother, Gytel, went through the school system's hierarchy to get the language changed. Eventually it was, though the school administration never quite understood Gytel's objections.

During the same period, a junior high newspaper included a full-page image of a cross to celebrate Easter. The principal of the school failed to recognize that image was not secular and could be construed as an endorsement of Christianity.

When Simone in 1969 refused to attend the required baccalaureate service on Sunday before her high school graduation because of its Christian nature, her principal threatened to not let Simone walk at graduation. She, in turn, offered to call the local newspaper and explain to them why a Jewish student would not be walking at graduation. The principal relented. A few years later, the baccalaureate service was made an optional part of the school's graduation program.

Rabbi Rita Sherwin, who arrived in 1992, has been explicit that at times she felt unwelcome in Springfield as a Jew. Moreover, members of the synagogue have had hate literature delivered to their homes—a phenomenon not uncommon in smaller, less diverse cities like Springfield. Instances of naive misunderstanding and overt bigotry such as these tend to reinforced that sense of alienation among those marginalized by the experience. Rabbi Sherwin believes, however, that Springfield is a "community striving to understand."[25]

CHAPTER II

Jewish Founders

German Jews in the New World

THE FIRST JEWS TO ARRIVE IN Springfield, Missouri were German Jewish merchants. These German Jews fled Germany between 1840 and 1880 for the same reasons as their Christian counterparts—the dire economic situation caused, in part, by war. They had a few added burdens as well. The laws in certain Prussian states forbade any but the firstborn Jewish son to remain in the parents' home community to keep the number of Jews in any one community within what was considered acceptable limits. Thus, if other younger sons hoped to establish a residence, a job, and ultimately a family, they had to leave. German Jews had three major advantages over non-Jewish German and Irish immigrants. First, they were literate, which made learning to read English easier. Second, they were peddlers who applied their knowledge to became merchants, rather than farmers seeking land that they often could not afford to get to. Third, they came with some money with which to begin to build a new life in their adopted country.

Since most Jewish immigrants were merchants in Europe, it was only natural that they relied on those skills they already possessed to become successful in the new country. Historian Hasia Diner explains that

> the less developed a region, the poorer the internal transportation
> networks, the fewer settled merchants present, the further the
> distance from one settlement to another, and the more agrarian
> the region, the more attractive immigrant Jewish peddlers found
> it. Certainly the southern region of the United States fits all of
> these criteria. The least urbanized part of the United States for
> the longest time, the most agrarian, and the one with the least
> articulated system of roads and railroads, it attracted Jewish
> immigrant peddlers well into the early twentieth century. In

31

the absence of focused case studies of Jewish peddling, let alone comparative ones, one can at least begin with the hunch that the South's persistent agrarianism, its fairly small commercial class, and its lag in industrial and urban development as compared to other American regions, made it a particularly attractive magnet for young Jews looking to gain a foothold in American commerce.[1]

However, not all Jewish immigrants were itinerant peddlers. Some went to small towns to establish themselves. This is far closer to what happened in Springfield.

German Jews in the United States retained good relationships with German Christians because, according to Michael Meyers, those "who took the initiative to leave Germany were less likely to have been under the influence of anti-Jewish prejudices than those who remained, and once they arrived most of them readily accepted the American value of social equality."[2] The relationships between the Christian Germans and the Jewish Germans were cordial because together they shared and celebrated a common heritage. Thus, even as German Jews scattered across the Midwest and South—often to become the first Jews in a community—and began the process of integrating into American society, conviviality of fellow countrymen allowed them to do so without abandoning their Judaism. As a result, German Jewish merchants were able to mobilize cultural familiarities to open stores in just about every town from the Alleghenies westward. Indeed, Jewish-owned stores became a ubiqitous sight in small town America. Frequently, the number of stores owned by Jews in a given community was out of proportion to their total population. The location of a railroad line was instrumental in the formation of far-flung Jewish communities. It provided access to merchandize in a timely manner—important to a merchant. This was true for Missouri, as we shall see the history unfold.

The First Jews Arrive

The first Jews to arrive in Springfield were Dr. Ludwig Ullman and his wife Sarah Maas Ullman. The passport of their eldest child Clara, indicates that they arrived in the city some time before 1864. It seems that Ludwig moved to Springfield from Sarcoxie (about 53 miles to the west), where he was listed in the 1860 census. What he did between his 1842 emigration from Germany and taking up residence in Sarcoxie remains a mystery, as

The southeast corner of Springfield's town square as it looked at the time of the Ullman family's arrival. *Courtesy The History Museum on the Square.*

does his reason for choosing to leave the small Missouri town. It may be that the doctor realized that Springfield was safer than Sarcoxie, because, as a border state during the Civil War, eruptions of military actions, irregular warfare, and feuding sent the region into constant disarray. Meanwhile in Springfield, in 1861, a soldiers' hospital had been opened, and Sterling Price wintered his eight thousand troops.

As most residents of the area were occupied in farming, there was not much to Springfield beyond the public square. Indeed, the telegraph had only just arrived in town four years prior to the Ullmans' move. The unfinished square was surrounded by wooden buildings that included general stores, bakeries, the stagecoach stop, and blacksmith. In 1861, the population of Springfield was estimated to be about 2,000. When the Ullmans settled in town, however, it was in the midst of a building boom. The roads, or mud paths, around the square "were a veritable jam of brick, mortar, lumber, stone and other building material."[3] They also arrived shortly before the ratification of the 1865 Missouri Constitution "that all men have a natural and indefeasible right to worship Almighty God according to the dictates of their own conscience."[4] As the Ullman family grew with the birth of three sons—Abraham in 1866, William in 1870, and Lee in 1874— the children were guaranteed an education in the Springfield by the new

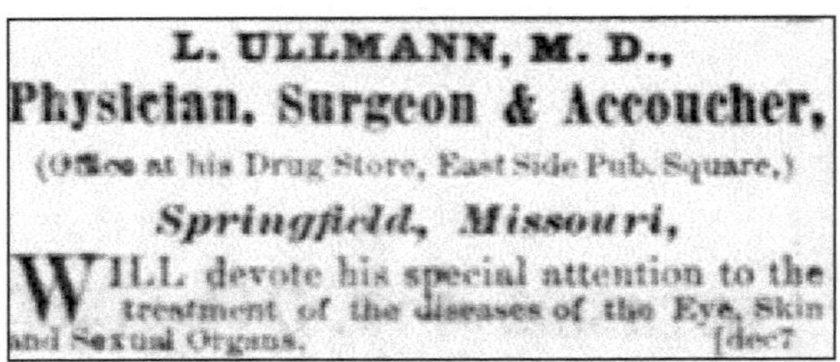

An 1867 advertisement for Dr. Ludwig Ullman's medical practice located in his drug store on the town square. *From The Missouri Weekly Patriot.*

state constitution's ninth article dictating that the Missouri General Assembly "shall establish and maintain free schools."[5]

As an 1861 graduate of the Pennsylvania Medical College, Ludwig Ullman opened a drug store and doctor's office on the east side of the public square where he specialized in "[t]he treatment of the diseases of the Eye, Skin and Sexual Organs."[6] Though the origins of the drugstore can be traced to the Colonial Period, the modern pharmacy developed, in earnest, in the 1860s. Previously, those seeking remedies for ailments relied on alchemists with little medical knowledge, or procured medicines directly from their doctors. Along with the medicines that Ludwig made, he likely sold some spices, tobacco, kerosene, fabric dye, perfumes and cosmetics, and the new patent medicines that became increasingly popular after the late 1870s. The list of medicines that Ludwig stocked would have included opium, morphine, ginger root, and cod liver oil. His arrival in the mid-1860s made him one of the first members of the Springfield Medical Society.

The city had become an organizing base for the local militia and military by the end of the Civil War, with the hospital for the Army of the Frontier in residence. Fortunately, Ludwig Ullman was around to minister to the people suffering during the 1866 famine that struck the region after a heavy frost killed crops.

He also helped his brother-in-law Dr. Abraham Maas get established in Neosho (about 74 miles southwest of Springfield). Together they invested in a drug store, much like Ludwig's.

At the end of 1867, State senator Gerhard Goebel commissioned the 22 member Greene County Board of Immigration to encourage settlement in the area. This was part of a statewide mission, as a state board was also appointed by the governor. Because towns were anxious to find workers to support the railroad industry, as well as settlers to develop "unused" land for agriculture, the state sought "to re-pair as rapidly as possible the losses of population sustained through the desolations of war."[7] Springfield boasted a

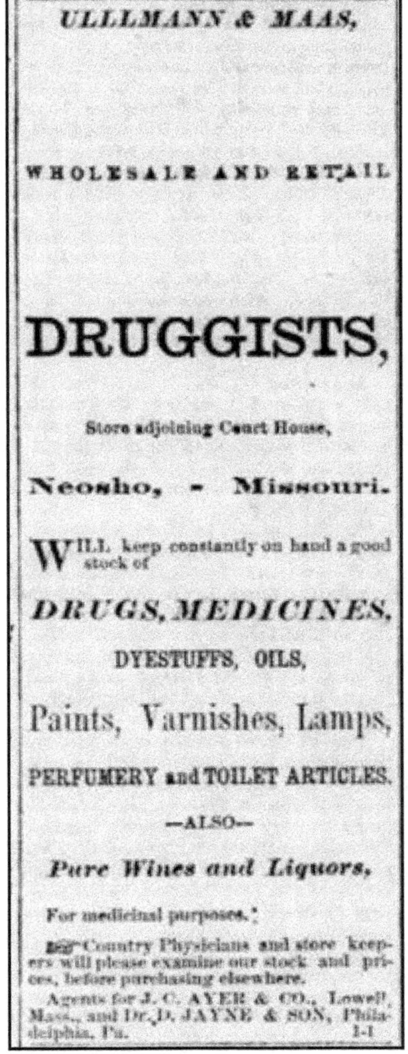

An 1870 advertisement for Dr. Ludwig Ullman's joint-venture in nearby Neosho with brother-in-law, Dr. Abraham Maas. *From the Neosho Times.*

population of 12,792 by 1868, almost exclusively white (less than 8 percent of the city was African American) and for a merchant this would be a tempting proposition. After the economic panic of 1873, the boards lost funding, and, by 1904, they had been decommissioned.

Sylvian Levy and his family (including his wife Caroline; daughter Leah; and sons Emile, Edgar, and Ferdinand), may have heard of the city through the work of the Greene County Board of Immigration. In April 20, 1868, *The Springfield Democrat* ran an advertisement for The Star Clothing House located behind the Court House. It was not until 1870 that it was disclosed that the Star Clothing House was owned by Sylvian Levy. Sylvian sold women's undergarments, like corset and bustles along with stockings and men's underwear. New factory-made clothes of women's blouses, skirts, and dresses and men's shirts, suits, and slacks were an important part of his inventory, as well accessories such as the hats and gloves required for the workplace. The family did not stay long in Springfield, however, as they had left by 1873. It was not uncommon for Jewish merchants to try a town and move on if they did not like the environment or saw better opportunities elsewhere.

A view of Springfield's public square, including Star Clothing House (second building from the left) and the Trade Palace (behind the water tower), circa 1870s. *Courtesy The History Museum on the Square.*

The German immigrants, Jewish and Christian, were generally well accepted in Springfield and the surrounding. In 1870, only 185 of the 21,550 residents of the county were German born. German immigrants represented a small minority scattered over the entire county, thus, they posed no real threat to the status of longer established groups. Frustrated that efforts in induce immigration to the area have not yielded results, business-oriented residents grew concerned about the physical state of Springfield. The main square remained underdeveloped, and the streets were often garbage filled.

An 1868 advertisement for the Sommer's Trade Palace. *From The Missouri Weekly Patriot.*

It was around this time, in 1868, that Victor Sommers (sometimes Summers or Somers) came to Springfield. Born in 1840 in Germany, he arrived in New Orleans with his parents David (or F.) and Sara Marks and five sisters. They traveled directly to Louisville, Kentucky, a hub for Jews on the western edge of the United States. As a businessman looking for an opportunity, the announce ment that a railroad would pass through Springfield enticed Victor to move west. Upon his arrival, he opened Victor Sommers & Co. on Boonville Street just north of the city square. The shop sold clothing and notions (like buttons and threads) for the entire family—an early department store.

In 1869, he returned to Louisville to marry Bertha Backrow (sometimes Beckrow or Bacron). The 1870 census records report six people living in the Sommers' household in Springfield, including the couple, Rose Bacherack, who was likely Bertha's younger sister. They were joined by two men, Julius David and Jacob Newman, who may have been store employees, and, finally, Bettie Butler, who, perhaps, was employed by the household as a domestic servant.

A New Decade

The Atlantic and Pacific Railroad opened their Springfield depot on May 3, 1870. Technically, it was not within the city limits, but north of it. Indeed, the area around the depot was eventually designated as the town of North Springfield. Fifteen years earlier, John S. Phelps, a former state representative and leading Springfield attorney, had first proposed the idea of a cross-country railroad with a depot in Springfield, but it was not until 1866 when the railroad received the land grants needed to begin construction. Most of the work done on the Atlantic and Pacific through Springfield was done by local labor. Phelps gave a speech at the grand event celebrating its completion explicitly stating that "[w]e were almost in an isolated condition; access to our country could only be obtained by days of tiresome and weary travel over rough and rugged road." He called the event "the morning of our prosperity."[8] The local newspaper described the arrival:

> The first locomotive that ever ascended the Ozark mountains made its appearance at the depot. The curiosity to see the first iron horse led a large number to the spot, and as the train approached long and loud huzzas rent the air and startled the genii of the place. Aged men and women, on the very verge of eternity, gazed for the first time on the object they had heard so much of had waited so long to see. Boys and girls just budding on the horizon of manhood and womanhood, who had frequently read in THE LEADER of railroads, the wonderful speed of the locomotive, its strength and usefulness, now for the first time behold its sinewy arms and muscular development, its graceful strokes and rapid evolutions. They gathered round and admired its well polished limbs [and] gentle manners. After quietly submitting to a close scrutiny from the crowd, it lifted up its voice and shouted with joy, much to the astonishment of the gazing multitude. It then gathered its strength and sped away like a sightless courier on the incorporeal bosom of the air.[9]

The completion of the railroad was a significant moment in Springfield history, as it brought a population explosion to the town. In 1868, the population of Springfield was 1,964, but, by the 1870 opening of the depot in North Springfield, it had risen to 5,555. In fact, between the 1868 and 1869 school years, another 431 children joined the school system. A decade later it grew to 6,522. Over the course of the next two decades, Springfield and North Springfield grew into a small city with 21,850 inhabitants.

It was quite common during this period for one member of a family to move to a new town and family members to follow. At the end of 1875, Victor announced a partnership with his brother-in-law Ferdinand Bakrow at his location on the north side of the square. While it appears that Ferdinand had been making a living selling life insurance, in the *1878 Springfield Directory*, he is reported as working at Victor Sommers & Co.

The Cohn Brothers' Store located on the east side of the square at the Boonville intersection in 1876. *Courtesy The History Museum on the Square.*

Why the Cohn and Backrow families followed the Sommers to Springfield is not entirely clear, but it follows that they were acquainted with one another and share similar motives. By 1881 there were only 3,000 Jews in Louisville, which tells us that in the 1870s there were far fewer. There was only one synagogue in Louisville until 1877, meaning that the families most likely worshipped together. Moreover, they may have known each other from Louisville's Young Men's Hebrew Association, which sponsored lectures and dances, providing Jewish residents—including the Sommers, Cohn, and Backrow families—opportunities to socialize.

The Cohn brothers, Julius, Emil, and George, arrived in Springfield by 1870, just before the opening of the railroad. Like Victor Sommers, the Prussian-born brothers had also been merchants in Louisville before making their move to the Ozarks. Their journey, however, began in New York City, where they arrived in the United States, before heading to New Orleans. The outbreak of yellow fever and cholera in the Crescent City forced the brothers to relocate to Louisville, Kentucky.

The Cohn family shared a single residence in Springfield according to the 1870 census that reported the household included Julius and his wife Sarah, his sister Julia (age 11), and his brothers George and Emil. The *1873 Springfield City Directory*, however, reveals that the Cohn business had expanded. Julius and George remained in Springfield, but Emil has relocated 60 miles to the west to operate a Carthage branch. Meanwhile, the family had been joined by another brother, Theo, who was running their store in Joplin. George was the buyer traveling to the East Coast to find the best prices and materials.

C. D. Hoffman is listed in the *1873 Springfield City Directory*, along with Victor Sommers as an owner in Victor Sommers & Co. Hoffman may have been Sommers' financial backer or silent partner because there is no listing for Hoffman in the city records. By 1875, Sommers was considered by the local press to be "one of [Springfield's] most enterprising dry goods merchants."[10]

North Springfield's railroad connection provided some clear economic advantages over their neighbors to the south. Even before the economic panic of 1873, the rivalry between the two had a detrimental effect on the Springfield's square as it fell into decline. To fix the situation, the cities agreed to build a streetcar line to connect the commercial hubs. Railroad executives, however, had over-extended themselves causing the failure of Jay Cooke's New York bank in 1873, sparking a nationwide economic downturn. I. Holcombe, a historian, describes the panic in his 1883 history of the county:

> The panic of 1873 had a more damaging effect upon Greene county than on many other communities in Missouri. "Hard times" set in the fall and continued until late in the following year. Money was scarce, the rates of interest exorbitant and usurious, while property of all sorts and kinds depreciated very seriously.

Lands in the county were indeed "dirt cheap" and lots and houses in Springfield sold for one-half of their former value. North Springfield was badly injured. Many persons disposed of their property at a sacrifice and left the county.[11]

Despite the depression, the Springfield Gaslight Company began business in 1874, and, by 1875, it had 82 customers and lit 50 streetlamps. In the following year, the company expectation was to have 40 more customers and 50 more streetlamps. Springfield had also added a dentist, a dressmaker, a jeweler, a watchmaker, tailors, a blacksmith, a baker, a butcher, and a stationer to its roster of business enterprises.

By 1875 another Cohn sister, Rachel, who was married to Morris Cohen, had moved to Marshfield, 26 miles northeast of Springfield. They were joined by their children Charles (age seven), Mattie (age five), Burtie (age three), and Lula (less than a year old), and, eventually, Joel who was born in 1878. The oldest two children had been born in Indiana, Burtie in Connecticut, while the youngest two were born in Marshfield. The penetration of rail into Southwest Missouri made the growing city of Springfield and the surrounding area an increasingly desirable destination for immigrants.

In 1878 Springfield was described as "the chief commercial representative of this section [of the country]" and it covered 240 acres of land.[12] The stores were built of brick by this time. The school system boasted 5,133 white students and 530 colored students with 113 teachers earning $38 per month for male teachers and $27 per month for female in 1877. In the next year, the railroad expanded north to Ash Grove, and, by 1881, the line ran to Kansas City.

Additionally, the city garnered even more prestige when Springfield College, later renamed Drury College and now Drury University, opened in 1873. The Association of Congregational Christian Churches had been looking to open a school in southwest Missouri, and Springfield competed with other towns in the area, like Carthage and Neosho, to be selected as the site for the institution. Significant community support, including financing, strengthened Springfield's bid. The opening of the college seemed to announce that town had matured into a real city *The Patriot-Advisor* described the city industrial base as including,

A large cotton mill, employing a hundred hands, makes thousands of yards of domestic and pounds of yarn and twine daily. A wagon

Fairbanks Hall on the campus of Springfield College in 1876.
Courtesy The History Museum on the Square.

factory, employing over fifty hands and the best machinery, is
making two thousand wagons a year, equal to the best made in
the United States. An additional factory makes from forty to
fifty wagons each year. The iron works employ over forty hands,
and turn out from forty to fifty thousand dollars worth of work
per year. The Eagle foundry, which does a large amount of work,
employs a number of hands. The woolen mill makes cassimeres,
jeans, blankets, flannels, etc., of as good quality as are made
anywhere; merchant flouring mills, which make an article of flour
that cannot be excelled; a planing mill and sash, blind and door
factory, which turns out the very best of work; tobacco factories,
whose best brands of tobacco have a wide reputation and meet
ready sale; cigar makers, who turn out yearly several hundred
thousand A No. 1 cigars, and medical laboratories, sending out
thousands of dollars worth of proprietary medicines, which are
rapidly becoming popular.[13]

Frances née Cohn and Jake Marx. *Courtesy Donald L. and Linda P. Cohn.*

Development in the region only enticed more Jews to move to the city, as expanding economic opportunities in the region's commercial and transportation hub drew more merchants and more economic activity.

In 1878, the Cohn brothers had a new partner—their brother-in-law Jake Marx. He had married their younger sister Frances that same year. Jake arrived in the United States in 1867 and moved to Louisville, where he met the Cohn family.

Meanwhile, Julius, Theodore, and Emil Cohn, along with Abraham Bloom, opened Cohn Bros & Co. in Cincinnati, Ohio. The Jewish community in Cincinnati was older and more established, as the first Jew had arrived in 1817. By the 1850s, the city was the hub of ready-to-wear men's clothing. Moreover, the Jewish community was comprised almost entirely of Germans, and thus, by 1878, had emerged as the center of the American Reform Movement—a German Jewish religious movement. Cincinnati was home to the Union for Reform Judaism, a congress of Reform rabbis from the south and Midwest, founded in 1873, and the Reform rabbinical seminary Hebrew Union College established in 1875. The Cohn brothers had moved from one burgeoning community to another. In 1880, Julius and Sarah are listed as boarders of Eli Oppenheimer in Cincinnati.

The 1880s

In the early 1880s, Springfield boasted a train depot, and a cotton mill, a woolen mill, and a flour mill. The railroad linked Springfield to Kansas City, diffusing some of the rivalry between Springfield and North Springfield. The two towns realized that cooperation might better serve their respective interests. There was a livery and a stable for the streetcar that ran from the old town to North Springfield. The city had two firehose cars and a ladder. There were fire hydrants, as well.

Gus Marx joined his brother Jake by 1880, as he is listed on the 1880 census record as living with Jake and Frances. Jake was quickly recognized statewide as a quality gentlemen's clothier. Gus was a salesman in the store and, later, the bookkeeper.

Both Ferdinand Bakrow (Victor Sommers' brother-in-law), listed as Ferdinan [sic] Bashrow, and his cousin Richard Bashrow were living with Victor and Bertha in 1880. By 1881, Victor Sommers & Co. had relocated to the City Hall Building on the Square.

In 1880, Springfield had a population of 26,009 whites, 2,808 non-whites, and 807 foreigners, although who was defined as a foreigner is unclear. The newly established connection to Kansas City opened economic and social opportunities. In 1879 or 1880, Daniel H. Herman, the son of New York German immigrants, arrived in the Springfield establishing a tailoring business on Boonville Street just north of the square. Holcombe notes that Daniel Herman's brother Charles worked with him

The German-born proprietors of Herman the Tailor, located on Boonville Street. *Courtesy Greene County Archives and Records.*

and ran the branch of Herman the Tailor on Boonville Street, in North Springfield. The brothers boarded at the Metropolitan Hotel in 1881, but by 1884, Charles had moved into Pahlman's Restaurant. Daniel, who was occasionally referred to as David, was praised for his honesty, good business sense, "excellent taste," and the fine quality of his workmanship. Charles must have been important as well, as the brothers' images are one of the few to be included in Holcombe's 1883 local history. The recognition is not surprising as they had two stores. Upon Daniel's death in 1926, the newspaper called him a pioneer to Springfield—an interesting statement given that the city had been established for at least thirty years before his arrival.

From Springfield, Missouri and Surroundings 1889

Despite owning property in Springfield, the Ullman family had moved to Cleveland, Ohio where Ludwig was a partner in Ullman-Philpot, an ink manufacturer. Cleveland was surely a more sophisticated city. In 1882, while the family was residing in Cleveland, Sara and Ludwig's eldest son Abraham died at only sixteen years old. The Ullmans returned to Springfield where they buried their son in the Hazelwood Cemetery. There was no Jewish cemetery yet, so they were forced to use the city cemetery.

The Metropolitan Hotel on College Street, where the Herman brothers resided in 1881. *Courtesy Springfield-Greene County Library.*

Immigrants continued to arrive throughout the 1880s, including the German Jewish immigrant Jake Rothschild. Born in the Rhine in 1860, he and his twin Simon came to the United States when they were eight years old. Jake moved to Springfield with his bride Julia Hirschland, after stops in New York, St. Louis, and Marshfield. It is likely that Jake became acquainted with Morris and Rachel Cohen in Marshfield and were, in turn, introduced to other members of the Cohen family from Springfield during visits. These encounters may have encouraged Jake's move to Springfield, where he made enough of an impression to be included in Holcombe's 1883 biographies of the city's important people, despite being only 23 years old at the time. His business located on the northside of the public square, Jake Rothschild and Co., was first listed in the *1884-5 City Directory*. When he opened his business, he sponsored a parade to celebrate. The opening ignited a rivalry with Daniel Herman so intense that Daniel threw clothes out of his store to distract parade watchers.

In 1883, Gus LeBolt came to Springfield where he worked in a mercantile. August "Gus" LeBolt was born in Piqua, Ohio in 1866. His parents,

Charles and Esther, were both from the Rhine region—his father from the French side and his mother the German. Charles moved from Pittsburgh, Pennsylvania to Piqua because of the many economic opportunities carried by the river traffic that moved down the Ohio. Merchants, Jewish and non-Jewish alike, were keenly interested in how people and products moved around the country. As rivers were explored and then exploited, merchants would move to burgeoning towns to provide goods and services for the people living in the area and traveling the waterways. According to a local history compiled in 1880, Gus was the owner of one of "the prominent grocery houses" in the county.[14] Additionally, he was a pioneering member of Anshe Emeth Jewish Temple in Piqua. Charles' son-in-law "Small Sam" Altschul promulgated the legend that Charles' father had been given the name Le Bolt (The Bold) by Napoléon for whose army he procured meat. There does not seem to be any truth to the history of the name, though Charles' father did work in Napoléon's army. While Gus did not stay in Springfield, his time in the city was important as the LeBolt family later became part of Springfield's history. He moved back to Ohio in 1904. However, he made his national name in the new national pastime of baseball where he was one of the first pitchers to throw a curve ball. His brother, Joseph "J. D.", later became president and treasurer of the baseball team in St. Joseph, Missouri.

In 1883, Ferdinand Bakrow traveled to Offenbach, Germany to marry Minnie Oppenheimer. The wealth of the Backrow and Sommers business in the early 1880s was such that they could afford to send a member of the family to Europe, indicating the prosperity that the city of Springfield could generate.

In 1884, Benjamin Hirschland, Julia Hirschland Rothschild's brother, moved to Springfield where he joined the family business, while his nephew Gus attended Southwestern Business College. Benjamin Hirschland was born in Germany in 1851, to Samuel and Helene. The family immigrated in 1865 and settled in Cincinnati. After finishing school, he apprenticed to a cabinet maker. Gus became Rothchild's bookkeeper and Benjamin's brother Charles immigrated in 1856, assuming a position as a manager at the cigar manufacturer Ellenberg & Company. Eventually, Charles became a partner in the cigar company.

In 1884, William Cohen opened a bookstore at 123 Public Square. It was still opened in 1888 but was no longer listed in the 1890 city directory. As with many businesses in many towns, little else is known of either

Hannah Cohn.
Courtesy Donald L. and Linda P. Cohn.

the businessman or the business. However, a bookstore in town would likely have provided materials for students all over the county, as a typical bookstore of the period carried not only books and stationery, but also slates and chalkboards, writing tablets, pencils, and quills and ink. It may also have carried dolls and other small toys.

In 1885, Gus Marx married Hannah Cohn of Louisville, one of Frances' cousins. It was not unusually for families to marry into each other. With Jewish men scattered across the Midwest in small towns that often had few, if any, other Jews, families helped the eligible meet and marry.

This seemed the time to marry, as Daniel Herman married the daughter of German immigrants, Nellie Langsdorf. Daniel's business was booming, giving him ample opportunity to travel regularly to St. Louis, where he might find his future bride. The following year he opened a branch of his tailoring business in St. Louis.

For a short time, beginning in 1885, Jewish merchants Jacob Rodecker and Samuel Cohen, along with their partner William W. Smith, owned Rodecker and Cohen on the square, although neither Cohen or Rodecker resided in Springfield. Both Jacob and Morris Cohen, Samuel's brother and Jacob's original partner, worked for Levy Brother & Co. in New York and then Leavenworth, Kansas. Morris had been drawn to Kansas during the Civil War, as he was among the defenders of Fort Scott against Gener al Sterling Price's 1861 advance on the garrison.

In 1866, Morris and Jacob opened Rodecker and Cohen in Fort Scott. In 1880, Samuel Cohen, not yet a partner, opened a branch of Rodecker and Cohen in Clinton, which would have been on the stagecoach line between Fort Scott and Jefferson City. When Morris died, he left his part of the business to Samuel, who returned to Fort Scott. News of Springfield's importance as a commercial hub must have reached Samuel, because he opened a branch in Springfield.

In April of 1886, Albert Silberberg was the manager of the Boston Store on the east side of the public square. The Boston Store was owned by Julius Adler Baer, a German immigrant who lived in Fort Smith, Arkansas. Albert was married to Lena. A May 1886 newspaper announced that "Mr. Albert Silberburgh [*sic*] and family are visiting at Fort Smith" for what appears to have been a wedding.[15] By the late 1880s, there were an estimated 15 Jewish families in the two cities, Springfield and North

Nellie Langsdorf Herman.
Courtesy Tom Rose.

Springfield, that comprised the Springfield metropolitan area.

Richard Backrow, a son of Dora and Moses Backrow, and cousin to Bertha Sommers, did not stay long in Springfield. In 1886, he opened his own business in Louisville, becoming prominent enough in the business community to be included in *A History of the Jews of Louisville, KY.*

In 1886, Jake Marx opened the Oak Hall Clothier in the same building as the Cohn Brothers business. He and his brother Gus specialized in men's and boys' clothing. Advertising in the *Springfield Negro*, Jake and Gus were something of an anomaly in refusing to discriminate based on race and inviting the patronage of African American clientele. African Americans tended to appreciate German Jewish merchants who were not viewed to be part of the racist establishment and, thus, were willing to permit the African American customers to try on clothes, use their water fountains, and even haggle over prices. The Marx brothers took to Article I of the 1865 Missouri Constitution that color was not a basis for discrimination.

A nineteenth-century version of the "pop-up ad" for the Star Clothing Company taking a water break. *From The History Museum on the Square.*

Simon Hirsch arrived in Springfield with his family around 1886. He had immigrated to the United States around 1863, but first appeared in the 1870 Toledo, Ohio census. In 1872, he married Ohio native Tina. By 1880, the couple was living ninety-two miles north of Springfield in Clinton with their four children—Fannie (born 1873), Minnie (born 1875), Levi (born 1876), and Charley (born 1878). There he produced and sold whiskey. The couple added James (born 1880), Rose (born 1880), Adolph (born 1883), and Isaac (born 1886). Whether Isaac was born in Springfield or Clinton is unclear, but the other three were born in Clinton.

The Trade Palace, which originally had been owned by Victor Sommers, before passing on to the Ferdinand Backrow, closed in 1886. Apparently, Victor Sommers borrowed $1,500 from Mr. L. Oppenheimer in November 1886, and by February 1887 Sommers owed over $4,000 on his merchandize and $1,516.17 to Oppenheimer. The sheriff was authorized to sell the goods to pay the debt. Albert Silberberg purchased the goods and promptly sold them to local consumers. Sommers' struggles had likely been caused by the Depression of 1882-1885, which was marked by a sharp decline in prices, even as production remained steady. Jake Rothschild was also hit hard by the depression. He was forced to shut his business in 1887 and return to his previous job of traveling salesman. Along with a branch of Herman's business in St. Louis eventually, branches in Lamar and Joplin; Fort Smith, Arkansas; and Dallas, Texas were opened. Their windows in Dallas were considered some of the finest to be seen in 1892. Although, the economic depression that had destroyed Victor Sommers & Co., it did not affect Herman the Tailor.

THE OLD RELIABLE

OAK HALL Clothing House!

Our Stock of MEN'S, YOUTHS, BOYS AND CHILDREN'S

SUITINGS & OVERCOATS

Are now in, and are second to none. We keep the best qualities and make the lowest prices.

JAKE MARX

Is Leader of Fashions and Maker of Low Prices. Call and see him.

COR. OF BOONVILLE STREET AND SQUARE

An 1890 Oak Hall Clothing House advertisement appealing to Springfield's African American population. *From The American Negro.*

Nor did the depression have much effect on the Marx brothers. In 1887, Gus traveled home to Germany for a summer visit, while in the fall their mother, Hannah Marx, came to Springfield to see Jake. The visit was recorded in Springfield's *Herald* which noted that Hannah "has not seen [her son] in twenty years."[16]

Along with practicing medicine, Ludwig Ullman invested in real estate. He considered Springfield a healthy climate for living and, thus, a promising location for investment. Among the numerous structures that the doctor built was the Ullman Hotel, on the southwest corner of Campbell Avenue and College Street. When it was completed in 1887, it was considered as one of the fanciest structures in Springfield.

Moses Levy opened The Model on the southwest corner of the city square in 1887, where it stood for nearly 100 years. Moses had arrived in Springfield with his wife Henriette and five children from Sedalia, where he

The elegant Ullman Hotel on Campbell Avenue and College Street.
Courtesy The History Museum on the Square.

already had a thriving business. He likely met Jake Rothschild in Marshall Township, where they were both merchants and part of the tiny Jewish community. Their relationship may have inspired Levy to eventually come to Springfield.

Moses originally joined his brothers David and Simon in business in Sedalia in 1864. The seventeen-year-old had landed in New York and set out almost immediately to see his brothers. David and Simon Levy opened their business sometime between 1861 and 1864 in Sedalia during the war. Sedalia was founded with the arrival of the Missouri Pacific Railroad in 1861. Connected to the East Coast, people rushed to region to build the community. The process was further stimulated when the Union Army took advantage of the railroad to establish its headquarters there, providing a merchant's dream location, as they could provision soldiers and their families desperate for goods, as well as the local populace for businesses to establish themselves.

David Levy was the buyer who returned to the East Coast to purchase new items for the stores. It was most likely during those trips that he met

Henriette Rosenheim who was to become his bride in 1873. Born in 1849, she was a native of Richmond, Virginia.

Two years later, in 1866, Moses was running the Levy brothers' Arrow Rock branch. In 1873, the Arrow Rock branch was moved to Marshall Township and was big enough to require two stores: one for general merchandise and one for clothing. During his time in Marshall Township, Moses was considered "a young man of energy, good character, and excellent business qualifications."[17] Simon joined the first volunteer fire company in Sedalia that began May 23, 1868, though it is unclear how long he continued this service to his community.

The first disaster to strike the Levi family was the great fire of 1868 in Sedalia that destroyed numerous stores, including Levy & Bro. The brothers had rebuilt by the end of the year spending $8,000 to do so. The second disaster struck the family when David died in 1883, leaving behind his wife Henriette and four children: Della, Theresa, Benjamin, and Mille. In a ceremony in Manhattan, New York, Moses Levy married his brother's widow Henriette Rosenheim Levy, in 1887, the same year he expanded into Springfield.

At least during the early 1880s, Simon was running the Nevada branch, which had gotten its first railroad connection in 1870. By 1881, there was a second line running through the town. The railroads were crucial to creating towns because they provided contact with other locations and the easy movement of goods. However prominent Levy & Bro. was in Marshall Township and Sedalia, the store's presence in Nevada was apparently not as important, as the 1887 official history of the town makes no mention of the business or Simon.

In 1887, the only son of Nellie and Daniel Herman, Edgar, was born. Though Edgar was first recorded in the 1900 census as Daniel's son, a 1908 news story reported that "Daniel H. Herman applied to be guardian of Edgar S. Herman, a minor."[18] The Springfield newspaper left no clue as to why Daniel was required to apply for guardianship of a young man who had been identified as his son. Even Daniel's obituary in the *Springfield Missouri Republican* says, "four children [Hortense, Blanche, Ruth, and Edgar] were born to this union [of Daniel and Nellie]."[19] Since no birth certificate is available, there is nothing to help clarify Edgar's relationship to Daniel and Nellie.

Business continued to expand, despite the depression. Albert Silberberg purchased the Boston Store in 1888, because Baer decided to devote himself

The Model on the square, circa 1910. *Courtesy Bob Piland.*

to his Fort Smith mercantile. Meanwhile, Jake
Marx hired his brother-in-law Herman Cohn
as a clerk.

The Jewish community continued to
grow. The first reference to the Weigle family appears in December 30, 1889, when the
Leader announced a "son born to E. Weigel
one of Herman's tailors."[20] In either 1876 or
1878, George, or Goodman or Guttman,
arrived in the United States. He was born in
Bohemia in the early 1850s. The 1880 census
shows Guttman living in St. Louis, Missouri
with the Dribens working as a tailor. One

Edgar Herman in 1893,
at the age of six.
*Courtesy The History
Museum on the Square.*

could presume Guttman chose St. Louis because there were already Weigles
living in the city as immigrants tended to live where they had family. The
most prominent Weigle in St. Louis was Abraham, a *mohel* (religious cir-
cumciser). He arrived before 1840 and opened a clothing store and helped
found the first Jewish congregation, thus more than likely Guttman was
related to Abraham in some way.

Kate Trawer arrived in the United States in 1878, and married Guttman
Weigle in 1883, in St. Louis. They had four children: Dora (born 1885), Ella
(born 1887), Benjamin (born 1889), and Hattie (born 1896). Ella became
the first person buried in the Jewish cemetery in Springfield in 1893.

Isaac Altschul moved to Springfield in 1889, at his father's behest, or,
perhaps, his bride Bertha LeBolt. In 1884, Isaac (age twenty-four) married Bertha (age eighteen). It is quite possible that the families knew each
other from when the Altschuls lived in Ohio. Her brother Gus had moved
to Springfield in 1883, and, by 1895, her brother J. D. was working for
Isaac. While their first child Jay was born in Ohio, their daughters Elsie
and Hortense were born in Springfield. The 1893 Goodspeed's *Pictorial
and Genealogical Record of Greene County, Missouri* described Altschul
thusly: "This gentleman is not only one of the leading business men of the
city, but is deservedly very popular. While he possesses a Hebraic name,
he comes from a family who have long been residents of America."[21] This
off-handed comment concerning his religious background was considered
more a statement of fact and the make-up of the community, than a nega-
tive statement.

Herman Cohn at age twenty-seven in 1889.
Courtesy Donald L. and Linda P. Cohn.

German-born Solomon and Julia Reinach fled to the United States after their elopement and settled in Cincinnati. By 1853, the Reinachs moved again to Pine Bluff, Arkansas, where their oldest Carrie, or Caroline, appears to have been born, though other records indicate all their children were born in Ohio. Nonetheless, the family did settle in Pine Bluff, Arkansas where Solomon's brother Isaac had established a store in 1852. Isaac was a prosperous man, while Solomon, who fought for the Confederacy, lost much of his property during the Civil War. He fought at the battle of Wilson's Creek, where he may have discerned the potential of Springfield. This foresight was amazing. Isaac, the younger, was a wholesale and retail alcohol dealer in Springfield in 1890. By 1892,

On the left, Dora Weigle, age eight, and, on the right, Benjamin Weigel, age four, in 1893. *Courtesy History Museum on the Square.*

Ella Weigle's gravesite in Temple Israel Cemetery. *Courtesy the author.*

The W. W. Smith clothing store also known as Star Clothing Company on the square in 1890. *Courtesy History Museum on the Square.*

his brother Charles joined him in business at the Kentucky Liquor House. Isaac became prosperous enough to be included in the *Pictorial and Genealogical Record of Green County, Missouri* which described him "as a man of integrity." The business was successful enough to support Isaac's brother Charles, who was described by Goodspeed as "energetic and efficient, . . . prompt and square in all his dealings."[22]

The 1890s

As the city of Springfield entered the last decade of the nineteenth century, it had a population of 21,850, including approximately 25 Jews from ten families.

The city limits extended from what is Market Street on the west to Benton Street on the east and just south of Cherry Street to Pacific Street on the north. The buildings in town were of stone, brick, and adobe. There were mills, bookstores, a gas company, and an electric company. There were a number of banks and saloons, along with a vibrant business district on the square and the railroad on the northern edge of town.

The growth of Springfield encouraged Henriette Levy, who had taken her family to live in St. Louis, to join Moses in Springfield. At this time, The Model was flouring on the northeast corner of the square. In 1891, Moses' brother Simon closed the business in Sedalia to join Moses in the Springfield business, sharing his home. It was at this point that Moses dissolved his partnership with Mr. Michael Weinberg.

Not everyone enjoyed the same kind of success. Jake Rothschild lost two lawsuits in 1890, as he was forced to pay Schwab Clothing $1,564 and $553 to Kamnixer, Prinz & Co. He lost another lawsuit in 1891, in which he was ordered to surrender $553 to the plaintiffs. Perhaps feeling the strain, in 1891, he took his brother-in-law, Benjamin Hirschland as a partner to keep the business solvent.

Other businesses could not stay afloat. The expanding city and growing population did not help Victor Sommers out of his financial straits. His brother-in-law sued for payment of accounts that Backrow had apparently turned over to Sommers. Backrow lost the suit, remaining in business selling lace curtains in the Central National Bank building as late as 1888. In 1890, however, *The Leader* listed him as living in St. Louis.

In 1891, Levy Brothers failed and Rodecker and Cohen, as partners in the business, were required to help pay the debts. It was shortly after this that the Springfield, Missouri branch changed hands, because the *1899 Springfield City Directory* listed William Smith as the sole owner of the Star Clothing Company, another name for Rodecker and Cohen. Additionally, the city brought a case against Albert Silberberg for obstructing sidewalks.

In 1891, Max Scharff, moved to Springfield where Max and Theodore opened a wholesale liquor business that they called M. Scharff & Bro. Shortly thereafter, they followed up by opening a retail liquor business as well. It is likely that they had some assistance from their cousins who owned the L. & A. Scharff wholesale liquor business in Springfield. The cousin may have suggested Springfield, with its vital rail line and burgeoning population, as a suitable site to start a new venture.

Born in Bavaria to a prominent family, Max Scharff had arrived in the United States in 1872 at the age of eighteen. Max's first job was in Vicksburg, Mississippi. His brother Theodore followed him to the United States around 1880, when they opened a business in St. Joseph, Louisiana. After their business was destroyed, the brothers took over the management of V. and A. Meyer & Co. that had four stores in Louisiana. In 1882,

Max married Rosa Scharff of Natchez, Mississippi. While she was born in Mississippi, as were three of her four siblings, her father Daniel Scharff, her mother Caroline, and oldest sister Bertha were all German immigrants. Max and Rosa had four children. The oldest, Daniel, may have been born in Mississippi, but the younger three, Clarence, Clara, and Fay, were born in Louisiana. In 1889, Rosa died and was buried in Natchez, Mississippi. *Goodspeed's History* described the brothers as "honorable men" and indicated that their business was "patronized by the elite of the city." In a creative way of acknowledging their Jewish heritage that to the modern ear smacks of antisemitism, *Goodspeed* noted that brothers came from "a thrifty, industrious and fore-handed Hebrew family," who "like the majority of their countrymen . . . have prospered in business."[23]

By 1892, the Marx brothers had split their business. Herman continued to work for Gus. After the death of their father Emmanuel in Germany, their mother Hannah moved to the United States to live with Jake, with whom she remained until her death in 1906. In 1893 or 1894, Gus moved his business, while Jake expanded. By 1898, Frances and Jake had become the owners of Marx Furnishings & Hat Company at 136 Public Square.

Nathan Balchowski, was a wanderer who settled in Greenfield, Missouri in 1894, believing that the railroad would pass through the town. Realizing that Balchowski was difficult for locals to pronounce, he changed his name to Nathan B. Nathan. He convinced Joseph Rubenstein, his brother-in-law, to join him that very year. Joseph Lewis Rubenstein was born in Russian Poland, which is now Lithuania, in 1872. He was studying to be a rabbi before he was slated to be drafted by the Russian army. In 1885, his parents arranged to send him to the United States. His older sister Etta Balchowski, Nathan's wife, lived in Illinois and was prepared take him in. Since he only spoke Yiddish, he wore his sister's name and address pinned to his coat, relying on strangers to assist him on his journey. In 1897, Joe married Rose, who had immigrated to Whiting, Illinois from a region of Austria that is, today, a part of the Czech Republic.

Albert Silberberg left the city by 1895, and, by 1896, the Boston Store was insolvent. Lena Silberberg defended her stock (she owned almost all of it) in the business in court, but court records made no mention of Albert, nor did they indicate where the Silberbergs were residing.

Ignace Glaser and his family were first listed in the 1895 city directory, which reported Ignace as being employed as a clerk at The Model owned by Moses Levy. Ignace was born in Austria in the 1860s and had immigrated

The Rubenstein family at their home in Greenfield, circa 1900.
Courtesy Rosemary Rubenstein.

to the United States in the 1880s. In 1893, he married Mattie, or Martha, Tinsley, who was born in Missouri in the early 1870s. They had one daughter, Elizabeth, who was born in Louisiana, Missouri in 1893.

By 1894, Daniel, Max Scharff's older son, had joined the family business, while Clarence, the younger son, was working in Vicksburg, Mississippi. Since Mississippi was where Max began his American experience, it is likely that the family maintained relations there. In 1895, Max Scharff married Carrie Hart in Cincinnati. Carrie's father Meyer was also a German immigrant. In Springfield, the family lived together: Max, his children, and his wife; Carrie's father and sister; and Theodore.

In 1894, the Marx Clothing Co. was incorporated by Frances Cohn Marx, Gus Marx, Julius Cohn, and others. Between 1895 and 1899, another Jewish business was opened by Jacob Goldring and Jacob Cohn, no seeming relation to the Cohn-Marx family. Together they ran a shoe store. What brought them to Springfield or from where they had come is not clear. Nor is it clear where they went when they closed the business. In 1896, Jacob Cohn married Minnie Longedon. J. D. LeBolt was working as a bookkeeper for I. Altschul, Jr & Co. starting in 1895.

The closing of the Silberberg's store circa 1896. *Courtesy Bob Piland.*

It is not until 1895 that Loeb, Benjamin and Charles Hirschland's brother who immigrated in 1865, was listed in the city directory as a clerk in Rothschild & Co. In 1898, both Ben and his brother Loeb were important members of the Jewish community in Springfield.

The Levy business was flourishing, as around 1896, Moses Levy moved his store to the east side of the square south of St. Louis Street. He was doing so well that on September 23, 1897, he threw a lavish wedding for his step-daughter Della. Both *The Leader-Democrat* and *The Springfield Republican* expansively covered the wedding of Della Levy and Abraham LeBolt, the brother of Gus and J. D. The Baldwin Theater orchestra played and Rabbi Leon Harris from St. Louis "performed the Hebrew ceremony in all its beauty and impressiveness" in the Metropolitan Hotel. The journalists were careful to note that "the banquet was one of the most elaborate ever served at the Metropolitan."[24] The guest list included the Jewish community of Springfield (the Marxes, Glasers, Rothschilds, and Altschuls, among others), Sedalia (the Wolfs), the Harts of Butler (also related to the Levys and Wolfs), and the Altschuls of Pine Bluff, Arkansas. The coverage a Jewish wedding received in the press was not unusual in small towns. Any major event was covered in the paper.

On the left, Della Levy LeBolt, and, on the right, Abraham LeBolt.
Courtesy Doug and Denise LeBolt.

The family experienced a loss, however, in the following month when Simon Levy passed away. Despite dying in Springfield, he was interred in Sedalia. The funeral took place in home of Henriette's brother-in-law Isaac Wolf, and was also presided over by Rabbi Harris.

In 1898, Max Scharff's son, Richard, was employed as a clerk in the family business. While Daniel Scharff married Elsie Althschul, the daughter of Isaac and Bertha, and opened the Parisian Store. Seeking one's spouse in the local community was not unusual. There delight in finding a Jew locally to marry was compounded by the guarantee that both the bride and groom could remain near their parents. By 1898, Frances and Jake had become the owners of Marx Furnishings & Hat Company on the Pub lic Square. Additionally, Nellie Herman was the treasurer of Herman the Tailor, while her relative, Henry Langsdorf, was the vice president. Final ly, Jake Rothschild had returned to his occupation as a traveling salesman, but, by 1898, he was the president and treasurer of the Rothschild Mercantile on South Campbell Avenue. Between 1898 and 1901, he became the owner of the Boston Trading Co. After 1901, the Boston Trading Co. changed hands again as it was owned by Albert Silberberg, who turned it into a department store.

In 1899, Moses hired his wife's nephew, Solomon Wolf, as a clerk in the store. Solomon's mother, Rebecca, recently widowed joined her son in Springfield, moving from Sedalia where the family business had been. Moses hired Solomon away from the Altschul brothers where he had been clerking.

The Founders in the New Century

The new century brought a period of regrowth after the depressions of the previous two decades. The city and its residents prospered.

By 1900, Charles Herman was no longer in Springfield as he appears to have returned to New York, while Daniel consolidated the business to one store on Boonville. Sometime after 1901, the Hirsch family left Springfield, moving to St. Louis. Victor and Bertha Sommers were recorded in the 1900 census as living in Hot Springs, Arkansas, residing the home of Moses Mendel, the husband of Rosa Backrow. In 1911, Victor Sommers died and was buried in the St. Louis's New Mt. Sinai Cemetery, while Bertha Sommers lived until 1921. She was buried in the Jewish Rest Cemetery in Hot Springs. Ferdinand Backrow, now Bakrow, became a partner in a business in St. Louis, Bakrow & Block Drapery, by 1893.

At the turn of the century, Solomon Altschul moved in with his son Isaac and daughter-in-law. By 1905, Charles and Ike were running a wholesale liquor company, I. Altschul Jr. & Co. The Jr. may have come about because Isaac's uncle in Pine Bluff was also Isaac. I. Altschul also became one of the charter members of the Bank of Willard. However, tragedy struck in 1901, when Charles' wife died. He later married Blanche. By the time of his death in 1922, Charles was vice president of the Citizens Mortgage and Security Company. Rabbi Samuel Thurman of St. Louis came to conduct the funeral service.

In 1905 Gus Marx was still involved in the men's clothing business, while Jake had begun to invest in properties. By 1912, Jake had become the president of the Springfield Life Underwriter's Association. The investment business was housed in the Woodruff Building, located a block east of the square, which opened in 1911.

Both J. D. LeBolt and his sister Hannah, or Nan, were listed in the *1905 Springfield, Missouri City Directory*, although they were not living together. J. D.'s business was among the first to rent space in the Woodruff Building.

The sons of Gus Marx, Jake, Gus, Jr., Arthur, and Emmanuel "Manny," along with Holland Chalfant and Gus Bowan, in front of the Marx Clothing and Shoe Store on St. Louis Street, circa 1916-1917. *Courtesy Madelynn Marx Inness.*

Additionally, J. D. was the president, treasurer, and secretary of the St. Joseph Saints—a minor league baseball team in the Western Association. When he died in 1917, he was buried in the Temple Israel Cemetery.

Tragedy struck the Levy family again in 1905, when Abraham LeBolt died from heart and kidney problems. The family had been living in Springfield, Ohio, where he ran both wholesale and retail cigar and tobacco businesses and dabbled in politics. He left his wife and three children, Mildred, David, and three-week-old Esther. His body was buried in the Jewish cemetery in Springfield, Missouri and Della and the children moved in with her parents.

Nathan B. Nathan moved on, sometime after 1901, as two of his children were buried in the Jewish cemetery—the second buried in 1901. Joe Rubenstein bought him out, turning to Marshall Fields of Chicago for credit against added stock. During the depression years, in a practice that was not uncommon among merchants at the time, Joe accepted barter. often in the form of butter and eggs, from customers who were farmers.

Because of the fifty-mile distance to Springfield from Greenfield, Joe had Friday night services at home with his family, and only attended congregational services with Temple Israel for the High Holy Days. Because he was traditional, Joe closed his store on the Jewish High Holy Days, which the locals respected. Nor would his employees accept payments on Saturdays—the Jewish Sabbath. The customers would come back another time to pay. Joe's compromise between American business practices and Jewish law was not unusual. Keeping of his store open on Saturdays, despite the Jewish prohibition of work on the Sabbath, was fairly standard practice across the South. When Joe died, the whole community attended the funeral, which was held in the school. He was buried in Temple Israel Cemetery.

Joe and Rose's son Arthur and his wife Thelma were married in 1922 and moved to Springfield. In 1924, they took over the Ullman Hotel, while the brothers, Arthur and Hershel, ran Rubenstein's in Springfield as a separate business to Joe's.

In 1906, Marx Netter married Rosa Abrams, who died two years later. In 1910, Marx married Fay Scharff, his boss' daughter, and moved to Springfield. Marx was born in 1872 in the contested region of Alsace-Lorraine on the French-German border. Prior to his move to Springfield, he managed one of the Max Scharff's plantation store. In 1903, he applied for a renewal of a license to sell liquor in Fayette, Mississippi.

In 1910, Marx and his brother-in-law Aubrey M. Ullman, who was married to Fay's sister Clara, purchased the Boston Store at forfeiture sale and reorganized the business. By 1917, it had been renamed Netter-Ullman Dry Goods. In 1922, Marx bought out Aubrey, who subsequently disappeared from Springfield.

In 1914, Ignace Glaser was recorded as the Levy-Wolf's vice-president. Between 1915 and 1921, he also served on the Board of Regents for Normal School District No. 4 (now Missouri State University). In 1925, he was made president of the board. Additionally, he became very involved in the Boy Scouts during the 1920s.

In his 1925 obituary, Jake Rothschild was described "as one of the leading merchants of this region," who had "become good friends" with Daniel Herman.[25] When Moses Levy died in 1928, the papers referred to him as a "pioneer merchant of Springfield . . . [a philanthropist and a business-man]."[26] Not only did the Associated Retailers of Springfield request stores to close in his honor as one of their members, but hundreds gathered at his home after the funeral.

Conclusion

While we may never know exactly what brought Ludwig Ullman, Sylvian Levy, and Victor Sommers to Springfield in 1868, we can speculate that these men, who were seeking a new and promising market, followed the progress of railroad construction closely and recognized the opportunity its arrival in Springfield presented. Though only Ullman realized immediate success in the up-and-coming Ozarks town, these pioneering German Jews were not entirely wrong in their assessment. Those who came after them did amazingly well. Solomon Altschul, a knowledgeable businessman, saw the potential during the Civil War. After witnessing the amazing growth the railroad sparked, he sent his son Isaac to share in the prosperity. He also saw to it that they established connections beyond the regions, sealing a relationship with the wealthy merchant LeBolt family of Piqua, Ohio.

Through the development of rail, the Jewish community established a merchant network in the Midwest that extended from the Ohio Valley into the Missouri and the Ozarks. The Bakrow family in Louisville, Kentucky had descendants in Springfield, Missouri and Hot Springs, Arkansas. The Cohn family had businesses in Springfield that expanded into Carthage, Joplin, and Marshfield, and, eventually, Cincinnati. The Levy family began in Sedalia, expanded into Marshfield, and, then, moved to Springfield. Finally, by marrying into the LeBolt family, the group expanded into Springfield, Ohio, solidifying their connection to the East.

It was through these family connections, the Levy-LeBolt-Wolf-Altschul-Scharff families, Cohn-Marx families, and Rothchild-Hirschland families, that the Jewish community expanded quickly and helped the town of Springfield grow into a city. As was typical for a South that was historically economically underdeveloped, it relied on outsiders to develop its urban markets. Trading on their own histories as merchants, Jewish immigrants often came to make up a huge proportion of a city's retailers. They did not, however, remain outsider, as they became integral members of the community in their own right—Springfield, as we shall see, is a case study of how American Jewish experience shaped the American experience.

CHAPTER III

The Second Community

Russian Jewish Immigrants to the New World

BETWEEN 1881 AND 1912, the largest Jewish group of immigrants arrived in the United States. Of the approximate 1,700,000 Jews who arrived, nearly 70 percent were described as Russian. These immigrants were fleeing the growing antisemitism in Czarist Russia, where they were not permitted to live or work outside the Pale of Settlement—a region between Russia and Poland that was severely overcrowded and provided poor agricultural opportunities. They were also restricted to certain occupations. Coupled with growing violence, life in the Pale had become unbearable.

Unlike the earlier German Jewish immigrants, most of these arrivals were poor, lacking education beyond instruction in Hebrew and religious law. Others were involved in socialist politics, some even rejected Jewish practice all together to study Russian and science, math, history, and modern literature. This created tensions within the American Jewish community. The established American Jews were mostly of the middle or upper class, had received secular education, remained observant of Jewish traditions, and had been accepted into their local communities. However, these established Jews were concerned that their social standing would be hindered because of their poor uneducated co-religionists and feared a rise in antisemitism. Additionally, the established community foresaw, because of the huge numbers of immigrants staying on the East Coast, under-employment and the resulting social and economic problems.

Organizations like the Hebrew Immigrant Aid Society (HIAS) and the de Hirsch Trust worked to assist immigrants through charity and relocation. These groups worked to spread out the immigrants so that they would not overwhelm any one community, thereby mitigating the potential expression of antisemitism that might follow a large influx of Jewish arrivals. Some communities in the Midwest saw opportunity for expansion by inviting these immigrants. The population of Jews in Missouri rose accordingly from nearly 8,000 in 1870 to 35,000 in 1900 to 50,000 in 1902. In 1912, an estimated 1,020 immigrants made Missouri their destination and 1,896 immigrated in 1914. With the start of World War I, the number of Jewish immigrants to the United States and, thus, Missouri, dropped dramatically to only 381 arriving in the state in 1915 and to 71 in 1916. Nevertheless, from 1880 to 1920, the Jewish constituency rose from 0.5 percent to 3.6 percent of the total U.S. population.

Tensions arising from the latest wave of Jewish immigration reverberated to divide the local Jewish communities as well. The new immigrants spoke Yiddish (a form of German written with Hebrew characters), while established Jews who were English and German speakers. New arrivals also followed a more traditional, or Orthodox, set of practices that the established community did not. Thus, especially in Midwestern small towns where Jews were settling, two congregations were often organized—a Reform and an Orthodox.

The First Eastern European Jews

Isaac Cohn, not related to the Cohn-Marx family, was born in Russia around 1875 and immigrated to the United States in 1889. His wife, Hannah Lorber, was born in Austria around 1875 and immigrated in 1890. They were married in 1896 in Whitely, Indiana where they remained until 1902. Their youngest child, Pauline, was born in 1904 in Kansas City. Though it is unclear why they came to Springfield, the growth the city experienced at the turn of the century may have been an enticement. The last record of the family in Springfield is the 1920 census, in which their household included boarders, William and Nathan Arbeitman.

The Cohn family were not the only ones to arrive around the turn of the century without any clear reason for their arrival. Joseph (sometimes Jake) and Marian Wennerman came to Springfield sometime before 1905, as their clothing business on Commercial Street was listed in the 1905 *Springfield City Directory*. Joseph was born in Russia in 1846. With his first wife, Frieda, he had two sons: Joseph, who died during the Great Influenza Pandemic of 1918, and Abraham, who lived in the Cherokee Indian Territory in the early 1900s. With his second wife, Marian (or Mary), also Russian born, he had two more sons: Samson (or Samuel) and Jacob, both of whom were born in St. Louis. In 1905, the couple adopted a little five-year-old girl, who they named Rossie. Other than the adoption record there is no information

View of the Springfield's square looking north, including Nathan Clothing Company. *Courtesy The History Museum on the Square.*

about this child in census records, cemetery, or death records. When Joseph died in 1922, Mary, Jacob, and Sam and the sons' children were listed in the will, but not Abraham or Rossie.

Abraham Winnerman[1] married Fannie Lobilsky twice. The couple were first wed in 1887, but they divorced two years later. In 1900, Abraham and Fannie remarried only to divorce again later in the year. Their marriages resulted in a daughter and a son. The daughter died before their 1900 divorce as Fannie testified in 1941. A reference in the local newspaper appears to confirm the death the child with the mention of the passing of "H. Winnerman," who must have been Abraham's since his was the only Winnerman family in the area. After the second divorce, she received custody of their son William and moved to New York City. By 1903, Abraham had married Golda. After spending some time living in Cherokee Indian Territory, the couple moved to St. Louis with their children.

Max, Lena, and their eight-year-old son Irving Washington Schwab arrived in Springfield about 1904. By 1909 *The American Hatter* described "Max Schwab [as] one of the leading hatters of Springfield."[2] How he knew that a hattery would do well in the city is not clear. Born in Germany in 1869, Max Schwab's father was a small landowner who raised cattle in the

The Schwab Brothers Clothing Company on South Campbell Avenue, circa 1908.
Courtesy The History Museum on the Square

Black Forest region, while Max was responsible for taking the livestock to market. Max immigrated to the United States in 1884, fleeing Germany to avoid conscription into Bismarck's army. Upon arriving in the United States, he worked in the garment district in New York City and studied English. From there Max moved to Huntington, West Virginia, where he worked for Jacob Zeigler. On the first day of 1896, Max married Jacob's daughter Lena, a native of West Virginia. While there is no record of the Schwab's business in the 1905 *Springfield City Directory*, there is a circa 1908 photograph showing their business, Schwab Brothers Clothing on South Campbell Avenue.

Max's brother David was born in 1871 or 1872. Their father was an abusive man who beat David with a whip, prompting him to follow his brother to the United States. Arriving in 1886, David worked as a traveling salesman, before he joined Max's men and boys clothing store in Springfield. David was tall, slender, good-looking man, while Max was a short, rotund, bald man. David, however, was an excellent poker player who had inherited his father's temper and would occasionally end up in fist-fights with the

On the left, Morris Moskowitz, and, on the right, Hannah Moskowitz. *Courtesy Mary Moskowitz Watters and Jim Watters.*

customers. Marrying late in life, David was nearly 40 years old when he wed his bride, Gertrude Simon, who was barely 18. Their marriage produced one daughter, Dorothy, born in 1909. Gertrude died in 1912. Her death devastated David. He only remarried because community members were worried about Dorothy's welfare. His second marriage to Dora Straus took place in Hamilton, Ohio in 1915. The Ohio native was the same age as her husband.

While the newspapers say the Moskowitz family arrived in 1912, they do not appear in the city directory until 1914. The family lived above Joseph Gold's grocery on Broad Street where Morris, Daisy, Sam, and Leo, the children, worked for their father. Ben another son apparently worked for the city fire department for two years where he drove the first fire truck with an engine. By the next year, Morris owned Atlantic Grocery Company and Sam and Leo clerked for their father.

The Moskowitzs both hailed from Hungary, Morris was born around 1864, while Hannah (or Chava) Neueman was born around 1867. They moved to the United States in 1886. Considering their ages—eighteen and nineteen respectively—they were likely married prior to immigrating. Indeed, family lore suggests that the couple wed in 1885.

They landed in New York, where Morris found work in Brooklyn as a tailor. The family remained in New York at least until 1902, as their first six children were all born there. In 1903, however, their youngest, Teddy, was born in Illinois. The family may have sojourned in Chicago for a while visiting Hannah's brother, Rabbi Morris Neueman. The move west had become a permanent arrangement, as, by 1910, the family had resettled in St. Louis.

Shoemakers

Julius Bookman was born in Russia in the early 1880s, immigrating to the United States just after the turn of the century. In 1911, he married Jean (or Jennie) Wasserman. Jean was born in 1891 and came to America in her childhood. The Wassermans lived in Ohio and Iowa before settling in Peoria, Illinois, where Jean met and ultimately married Julius. In due course, Julius and his bride found their way to Springfield where he started a shoe business on State Street.

Photographs exist that reveal that Mike Sussman worked in Julius Bookman's shoe store as early as 1912. The earliest official record of Sussman in Springfield, however, is his 1917 registration for military service, in which he listed his mother, wife, and daughter as dependents and reported that he had a "crippled ankle."[3] Mike, his wife Rose, and daughter Frieda had all been born in Poland—Frieda as late as 1910. Census takers recorded Mike's immigration date as 1911, when he most likely arrived in Galveston, Texas, where Russian Jews were often transported. From there, the HIAS placed Mike with Bookman. Rose and Frieda did not make the journey to the United States until 1916. Their long separation was not unusual as men often came in advance of their families in order to saved the money required to bring them over. Mike owned the Popular Price Shoe Store after working for Julius Bookman.

Israel Lotven was born in Russia in 1881 and lived in Rozebeh (also known as Grosoff), where he was occupied as a shoemaker. He married Charna in 1900. Like her husband, Charna had been born in Russia in 1881. The couple produced six children. In 1904, with the outbreak of the Russo-Japanese War, Israel Lotven decided to leave his family to avoid conscription and come to United States. His wife and children were supposed to follow shortly thereafter. Israel planned to take a boat from Germany to Ellis Island where he intended to meet his brother. Instead, the boat he took brought him to Galveston. He landed in 1912, and, like Mike Sussman,

HIAS placed him in Julius Bookman's shop. Israel only worked for Bookman for four months before venturing out to start his own business.

The Scrap Metal Men

Benjamin Karchmer had traveled through Springfield a number of times before making the Ozarks his home. After some encouragement from neighbors who had previously lived in Springfield, he moved his family to the growing city, where he opened Karchmer Iron & Metal Company in 1912. The collecting scrap metal was the family business as both of his brothers owned similar enterprises in St. Louis and Oklahoma City. Benjamin had been born in Vilna, in what his now Lithuania, in 1873, while his wife Anna (or Jennie) was born in Eastern Europe in 1878. They immigrated to the United States around 1890. Before coming to Spring field in 1912, the couple lived in Mississippi where their eldest child Jake was born in 1896. From there, the family moved to St. Louis, where their second son Nathan was born in 1899. Benjamin ran a furniture store in St. Louis until 1904, when he moved the family to Dallas, Texas. By then, the Karchmers had three daughters. The family remained in Texas only a few years before returning to St. Louis ahead of their move to Springfield.

Israel Lotven, Mike Sussman, and Julius Bookman outside Bookman's shoe store in 1912. *Courtesy Gytel Lotven.*

William and Nathan Arbeitman first appear in the census in Springfield in 1920, boarding with Isaac and Hannah Cohn. They arrived in the United States in 1912, however. The Arbeitman brothers were born in Russia about 1897 and 1900, although their tombstones give their birth dates as 1884 and 1882 respectively. They fled their homeland when soldiers warned them that a major war was coming, and that the brothers should leave to avoid being swept up into the conflict.

William had in-laws in Joplin who sponsored the two brothers. William had been a shoemaker in Lublen, Poland, prompting the family set up the brothers with a shoe store. When the brothers first opened their store, they shut on the Sabbath and the Jewish High Holy Days, but by the time their families arrive they only shut on the High Holy Days. According to Fannie, Nathan's daughter-in-law, the brothers "met a man in Joplin that had a shoe store in Springfield. So he brought them to Springfield!"[4] The shop owner was omnipresent Julius Bookman, the region's shoe entrepreneur.

The First World War

In 1914, David and Max Schwab built apartments on East Walnut Street for $30,000. They bought property on the Square and on Campbell Street. That same year, Israel Lotven brought his daughter Fannie to the United States to help earn the money needed to bring the rest of the family over. Throughout World War I, Israel had no contact with his family in Russia, who were suffering terrible privations. Though he registered for the draft in compliance with the Selective Service Act of 1917, he was never called up.

Rabbi David Lefkowitz, in a letter to the *American Israelite* in 1917, reminded Jews across the nation that "in all the wars of America, the Jew gave good account of himself, sending more than his quota to fight for the flag . . . the American Jew [will] fight loyally for the one land whose history has not been smirched by religious persecution of discriminatory laws."[5] Vulnerable as potential targets of ethnic bigotry, and, indeed, inspired by

Max Yoffie. *Courtesy Paul Isbell.*

their own love of country, Springfield Jews in great numbers enlisted, or registered for the draft, prepared to defend their adopted nation.

In 1914, Max and Lizzie Yoffie moved with their five daughters and one son to Springfield. Max was born in Amsterdam, Holland in 1872 to Nathan, who was a Sephardic (Spanish heritage) Jew, and Rebecca Burrik, a Jew from Lapland. His parents moved to Russia, where Max worked for Baron Rothschild. In 1889, Czar Alexander III threatened Jews with exile to Siberia, so Rothschild paid for all two thousand of his employees to immigrate to New York City. In 1893, Max moved to Forrest City, Arkansas after a stint in Memphis, Tennessee. In 1896, he married Lizzie Apt. Their son Samuel, meanwhile, served in the infantry during World War I.

According to his World War I draft registration papers Samuel Kemp took up residence in Springfield at some point before 1917. At that time of his registration, he was clerking for the Wennerman Brothers. Samuel Kemp was born in Manhattan, New York in 1883 to Morris and Augusta (or Goldie) Kemp. It is unclear where his parents were born as his birth certificate says Poland, while the 1900 Census say Russia and Germany respectively. Because the borders changed and census takers often guessed at place of origin when they were unable to understand the accent of the person they were interviewing, the answers may be entirely correct, regardless of the discrepancies.

In 1916, Ben Moskowitz was engaged in auto repair before moving on to work as a chauffeur, resuming the occupation he had in St. Louis. In 1917, at the age of twenty-nine, Ben was drafted into the army and was sent to Fort Riley in Kansas. That same year Hannah died of kidney disease in St. Louis. The Moskowitz family then moved back to St. Louis to be closer to kinfolk.

Census takers recorded Benjamin Ellman of St. Louis as unmarried in 1910. By 1917, however, he was living in Springfield and had married to Lillie. Born around 1880 in Russia, Benjamin had immigrated to the United States in 1893. His wife, Lilly Nudelman, was born around 1880 in St. Louis to Russian Jewish immigrant parents. Benjamin traveled for business, until he decided for some unknown reason to move to Springfield. In Springfield, he worked in sales helping businesses close. Benjamin also had a brother David and sister-in-law Esther who joined him in Springfield. David was a jeweler and opened a shop on College Street next to his brother's business.

In 1917, Julius Bookman moved his family to Picher, Oklahoma on the Kansas-Oklahoma-Missouri border. Realizing that he had better

On the left, Benjamin and Lilly Ellman. Top right, David Ellman. Bottom right, Jacob and Samson Wennerman. *Courtesy Marlita Wennerman Weiss.*

opportunities to the west, Julius went on to build the largest shoe store in northeastern Oklahoma. He had sold his Springfield business to Israel Lotven, who had secured loans from the shoe manufacturer Oscar Bloom and the Schwab family in order to finance the deal.

Joseph Wennerman ran a shoe business in Springfield on Commercial Street. Samson Wennerman attended Drury University and then Washington University Medical School, from which he graduated in 1915. He supported his studies by running a costume business with his brother Jacob. During World War I, Samson served as a surgeon and was stationed in Camp Dix in New Jersey and Fort Des Moines, Iowa. After the war, Samson moved to St. Louis where he became a surgeon. Jacob remained in Springfield and ran a clothing business on South Campbell Street.

Both Nathan (also known as Bill) and Jake Karchmer were drafted to serve during the war. Jake was sent overseas and returned by the end of 1917. Nathan, however, never served as the armistice was signed before he

On the left, Jacob Karchmer, and, on the right, Samuel Yoffie.
Courtesy Special Collections and Archives, Missouri State University.

Irving Schwab. *Courtesy Special Collections and Archives, Missouri State University.*

was scheduled to report for duty. After the war, Nathan and Jake opened an auto salvage business.

In 1917, Irving Schwab was drafted after his first year at Drury College (now Drury University). After the war, he finished college and graduated from law school to become the only Jewish lawyer in Springfield. Even

The D. M. Oberman Manufacturing Company Building on North Boonville Avenue.
Courtesy The History Museum on the Square.

though he was not generally observant, he did serve as president of the Reform congregation.

Jacob Wennerman died at the age of 29 in 1917, leaving his wife, daughter, and sister-in-law. Samson was appointed guardian of Fannie Gertrude Wennerman, who was only five when her father died.

Factory Work

David M. Oberman began his company in Jefferson City where he built a factory to employ prison inmates to make overalls. It was here that Jake Kransberg began working manager at the Oberman plant that opened in 1917. By 1926, Jake was considered by the local press as "one of the best factory managers in the state."[6] During the 1930s, it is estimated that the Oberman factory employed more the 50 percent of the Jews in Springfield.

Jake and his wife, Anna Gellman, were both from Russia, while and their three children, Sol, Mollie, and Morris were born in Missouri. According to 1910 census records for St. Louis, Anne had immigrated in 1892, while Jake had in 1895. However, Jake fulfulled his obligation to register for the draft, he did not become a naturalized citizen until 1928.

Jake brought his brother Fred (or Edward) and Sarah, Fred's wife, with him to Springfield. Both were born in Russia in 1896. Edward immigrated to the United States in 1912 from Swouivitch, while Sarah followed a year later. According to his draft registration, Edward worked as a cutter for Oberman's. Sol, one son, grew up and became a member of the St. Louis Symphony and Morris, the other son, ran a café in Springfield.

The Kranzberg brothers were later joined by sister Ida and her husband, Max Breadman, in 1918. Ida and Max were accompanied by their two daughters: Fannie and Bertha. Max worked as a furniture dealer.

Lottie and Ben Moskowitz in Kansas. *Courtesy Mary Moskowitz Watters and Jim Watters.*

Nathan Samors had come to Springfield from Chicago by 1918. At the time, Harry, Nathan's father, was working for William Seigel & Co. They shared their house with Harry's wife Bessie and their other son, Joe. Both Harry and Bessie were Russian born, while the boys were born in Illinois. Although the earliest city or federal documents suggest that the family had not arrived in Springfield before 1919, that the Samors were charter members of the Orthodox congregation indicates their presence in 1918.

After the Great War

In 1919, Ben Moskowitz was honorably discharged and in 1920 Morris died in St. Louis. Ben and Lottie Nichols married in June of 1920 in Kansas. The two had been neighbors in Springfield and despite their seven-year age difference had spent much time together. Ben had always been interested in cars and, so, in 1920 he and Lottie returned to Springfield where Ben started National Auto Company.

In 1919, Samuel Kemp divorced his first wife Eura who he had married in 1913. He rather quickly remarried to Austrian-born Edith, who had immigrated in 1906. At the time of the 1920 census, the couple was living with Jake and Mary Wennerman.

In the 1920s, Irving Schwab attempted a run for the state legislature. His political aspirations, however, came to an end soon after the Ku Klux Klan appears to have threatened him.

In 1921, fearful that his sons Isador, Jacob, and Chaim might be conscripted, Israel Lotven arranged for smugglers to get his family out of Bolshevik Russia. Jenny carried with her all her earthly possessions—her copper candlesticks, and her husband's *tallit* (prayer shawl) and Bible. Not wanting his family to live in a community that was not traditionally Jewish, Israel met them in New York where he tried to make a living. Quickly realizing that this would not work, however, he brought his family to Springfield, buying back the shoe business he had previously sold.

The family lived in the store for a month before Israel bought a house. The owner, Dr. Armstrong, and the bank provided the loans to make the purchase possible. In 1924, Israel became a naturalized citizen.

In 1921, Esther Ellman took her three children with David and ran off to Vancouver, Canada with liquor store owner Robert Tinkler. David was devastated.

Benjamin "Ben" Sussman and family moved to Springfield after 1921, so Ben could join his brother Mike's shoe business, working as a shoemaker. Mike Sussman

Israel and Jennie Lotven in 1922. *Courtesy Gytel Lotven.*

filed for bankruptcy in 1926, and the family moved to Detroit to make a start fresh.

Benjamin Sussman was born in Poland in 1888 or 1889. He immigrated to the United States in 1910. He met his wife Eva, who had emigrated from Poland in 1909, in New York City. According to the 1920 census. the couple lived in Brooklyn with their three-year-old daughter, Florence. Benjamin died in 1941 from a fall from the roof of his shoe store. His younger daughter Ruth, who had been born in Springfield, was just about finished with college.

In 1923, Ida and Max Breadman moved to Chicago, where they had their third daughter, Edith. Max's ill health, however, brought them back to Springfield in 1925, and, in 1926, Max committed suicide. The following year, Ida gave birth to the couple's son—Max. Although naming a child after a deceased relative is tradition among Eastern European Jews, naming a child after a person who had died young or with a mental illness is rare.

According to the local newspaper, Nathan Samors married Mildred Gordon of Chicago in "a very pretty church wedding . . . at Share Zedeck [*sic*] temple" in 1923.[7]

In 1927, Ed Kransberg became president of the DeLuxe Motor Company and moved back to St. Louis with his wife and three sons—Melvin, Herman, and Saul.

When Ben Moskowitz died of a brain-hemorrhage in 1930, just after his fortieth birthday, Lottie took over the automobile repair business. She had been the bookkeeper, so she knew the business well and both the employees and customers were loyal.

Benjamin and Lillie Ellerman had one daughter, Zelda, who was born in 1903. By 1930, they had moved back to St. Louis.

When Ida Kransberg Breadman died in 1931 of influenzal pneumonia, her oldest daughter Bertha, twenty years old at the time, became head of the house. None of the Kransbergs were buried in the Jewish cemetery in Springfield. Instead, they were transported back to St. Louis and buried in the Orthodox Chesed Shel Emeth Society cemetery, which was founded in 1888 as a burial society. There numerous Kransbergs are buried.

Conclusion

Unlike the first group of Jewish arrivals to Springfield, arrivals in this second wave were less likely to be related, or, even to be familiar with one another. Some were sent to Springfield by national organizations helping them find work, and others came of their own accord. However, the city at the turn of the 20th century was growing and offered these poverty-stricken immigrants opportunities to thrive and become involved citizens. These families jumped at the opportunities they did not have in their native countries. Their children went to school, they fought in the military as equals (even before gaining citizenship) and became naturalized citizens. These few Jews expanded Springfield's economy and society. They not only built businesses, but joined civic groups, provided charity, and became part of the culture of the community.

CHAPTER IV

Creation of a Religious Community

IT TOOK TIME FOR JEWISH COMMUNITIES to become formalized, but that was an important step for them to become a recognized part of the community. It provided for the Jews a way to gather and find strength not only for religious practices, but also as a political force. It also provided a type of community that their Christian neighbors were accustomed to and this provided a bit of legitimacy for Jews. Formalization came in two parts: a congregation and a cemetery. Sometimes these happened together like in Springfield.

First Congregation

Jews in Springfield began formally organizing in 1891, when Temple Israel placed an advertised in *The American Israelite* announcing the community's search for a rabbi. In November 1893, Jake Marx, Moses Levy, Simon Levy, Jake Rothschild, Daniel Herman, Benjamin Heirschild [*sic*], Jake Alschul [*sic*], and Theodore Scharff signed the Articles of Association for Temple Israel, making it one of the Jewish congregations in the state in 1900.

The new congregation took itself quite seriously. Even before it was officially recognized by the state, Temple Israel brought in speakers to underscore the role that Jews were having in American society. The first such speaker was Rabbi Henry Berkowitz of Kansas City who came

A December 1891 advertisement placed by Temple Israel seeking the services of a rabbi. *From The American Israelite.*

One of the signers of the 1893 Articles of Association for Temple Israel, Moses Levy. *Courtesy Doug and Denise LeBolt.*

in March 1892 to speak to the entire city at the Cumberland Presbyterian Church on "The American Jew." Berkowitz made sure to emphasize that "the mission of the Jew coincided with that of the American" because both focused on freedom and fairness.[1]

By 1907, Temple Israel boasted 132 members in a county with nearly 64,000 residents. Unsurprisingly, the congregation followed German Reform Jewish liturgical practices, as all of the members were German immigrants, or the children of German immigrants. Reform Judaism had begun in Germany in the late 1700s and came to full bloom in the 1800s in the Unit ed States. The Reform Movement in Germany pushed for prayer in the German language, rather than in Hebrew, so that congregants could understand religious services. Additionally, the movement advocated more liberal interpretations of the Jewish laws that would permit adherents to more easily integrate into the wider community. Prayer in the vernacular translated to the adoption of English over German or Hebrew in small town America. By 1918, the congregation listed its language of services as English.

Since a rabbi was not required to conduct worship, any capable adult male could step in to lead religious services. Thus, Jake Marx led the services at Temple Israel for over 20 years, becoming one of the many Jewish lay leaders that shepherded communities throughout the American West. Their lay leadership was instrumental to the vitality of American Jewish community in as much as there were only 22 ordained Reform rabbis in the entire United States by 1880.

In 1907, Rabbi Jacob Pollak of Newark, New Jersey was hired to lead the High Holy Day (*Rosh Hashanah* and *Yom Kippur*) services, which were opened to the general public. When, in 1915, the board of directors again considered hiring a rabbi for the High Holiday Days, the proposal was rejected. The cost may have been the deciding factor. Instead, member Isaiah Lerbover was paid to deliver sermons at the services, which he continued to perform on various Friday nights thereafter. However, in 1917 Rabbi Samuel J. Harris from Hebrew Union College was engaged to lead the High Holy Day services, impressing the congregation enough that it desired to bring him back in 1918. In 1919, funds were gathered to bring Rabbi Iparrell in to perform the honors. The practice of hiring a rabbi for the High Holy Days continued for many years.

The lack of a rabbi apparently became an increasingly pressing concern. In 1919, the board of directors decided to invite a rabbi to visit the congregation "to give us one or two lectures a Month [*sic*]." Rabbi Garry August of Joplin was formally invited "to come . . . every two weeks on Sunday night" to deliver a speech.[2] Only two months later, however, the series was cancelled.

Temple Israel joined the Union of American Hebrew Congregations (UAHC) in 1904. The UAHC had been founded by a synagogue president, Moritz Loth, in 1873, as it functioned as an umbrella organization to aid Reform synagogues with religious and social matters. Temple Israel was one of the 144 member congregations documented in 1905. As a community on the border of the American South, it was typical in that nearly 73 percent of early southern Jewish communities were aligned with the Reform Movement.

Second Congregation and First Rabbi

On December 21, 1918, the Orthodox community, made up of Jews from Eastern European, incorporated as Sha'are Zedek (meaning Gates of Righteousness). About 30 families had been gathering to worship together since 1912, and became the 51st Jewish congregation in the Missouri—up from the 29 that existed just 18 years earlier. The great influx of Jews from Eastern Europe was the impetus for the growth in the number of synagogues. Indeed, the Jewish population in Springfield rose 165 in a city of 39,631 with the county population around 68,000. Meanwhile, the Jewish population in the entire state had swelled to over 80,000, or about 2 percent of the whole. Hailing from Eastern Europe, the members of Sha'are Zedek had not been affected by the emancipation that had extended social and political rights to German Jews. This wave of immigrants therefore adhered to a different set of customs than their Reform co-religionists. For instance, prayer was conducted exclusively in Hebrew, the holy language, and men and women sat separately. At some point, the Orthodox congregation did away with gendered seating because, as Nathan Karchmer explained, the women "were respected. And we didn't feel they oughtta [sic] be separated."[3] This was not uncommon in small-town Orthodox congregations. Gender segregation in Orthodox synagogues was based upon the idea that during prayer men should not be distracted by women. The men on occasion would bring their children with them. In the front few rows these men would pray with their hats on, while the children sat in the very last row.

The founding families of Sha'are Zedek included the Arbeitmans, the Cohns, the Ellmans, the Epsteins, the Friedmans, the Golds, the Kransbergs, the Karchmers, the Kemps, the Leibowitzs, the Lotvens, the Luries, the Moskowitzs, the Rosenthals, the Rubins, the Samors, the Sussmans, the Sykes, the Wennermans, and the Yoffies. A pattern of informal gathering before becoming an incorporated organization was common to both Reform and Orthodox congregations. Since Judaism does not require any particular kind of space for prayer, these first congregations often met in people's homes or spaces rented from local businesses. For instance, the congregation frequently worshipped above the Chickering Piano Store.

There was a feeling among members of the Orthodox community in Springfield that the Reform community looked down on them. The two communities, therefore, minimized their interactions until the mid-1940s. This separation of the German and Russian Jews was fairly standard. The Orthodox Eastern European Jews did not like the Reform philosophy or practices, like men and women sitting together or the use of choirs and organs and felt that not praying in Hebrew disavowed the use of prayer because in the Orthodox view Hebrew is the holy language that is used for prayer. There was the added concern among the small-town German Jews that they were established and middle class and accepted and these newcomers might behave improperly. This coupled with the established family ties and cliquishness created animosity among the Russians toward their German co-religionists.

There were instances of detente, however, as Jacob Wennerman was a member of Temple Israel from 1914-1915. and rejoined in 1917. Ben Karchmer joined in April 1916. These men were examples of the rare traditionalist who was willing to compromise his traditional religious practices to join the only existing Jewish congregation. Most preferred to attend the type of services with which they felt most comfortable

Rabbi Jacob Lipman. *Courtesy Lorraine Lipman Raskin.*

One of the religious leaders of Sha'are Zedek was Benjamin Karchmer. He was responsible for recruiting Rabbi Jacob Lipman to move to Springfield from Philadelphia to become the community's rabbi, as well as the *shocket* (ritual slaughterer).

The Lipman family, including Jacob, his wife Dora, and their four youngest children, arrived in Springfield in 1923. Apparently one of the rabbi's first official duties was to officiate at the marriage of Mildred Gordon and Nathan Samors in 1923. The first listing for Jacob and Dwora (Dora) Lipman is in the *1925 Springfield, MO City Directory.* Their arrival coincided with another significant increase in Jewish immigration to Missouri. During 1920, over 1,100 foreign Jews immigrated to the state, while over 2,700 made the journey in the following year. When Rabbi Lipman died in 1933, Sha'are Zedek continued without the services of a rabbi.

Religious School

The desire for a religious schooling in Springfield was evident long before the first Religious School was finally opened. In 1875, Miss Clara Ullman, daughter of Dr. Ludwig Ullman the first Jew in Springfield, wrote

The first Religious School class photograph in 1893.
On the back row, from left to right, Fay Netter, Clarence Scharff, Edgar Herman, Ray
M., Mrs. Hattie Cohn, Dan Scharff, Clara Hirsch, Leo Ellenberg, Hortence Herman.
In the front row, from left to right, Dora Weigle, Irving Levy, Jay Altschul, Ben Weigle.
Courtesy The History Museum on the Square.

to *The Sabbath Visitor* that she was "outside of the Jewish ring" and "truly jealous of the pupils" who attend Jewish religious schools.[4] First published in 1874, *The Sabbath Visitor* was a periodical that provided Jewish religious lessons and advice, puzzles, and more to Jewish children around the country. The issues were often passed around an entire community. Miss Minnie Hirsch was the fourth reader of the Springfield copy.

The first Sunday School began in the summer of 1888. Ed Greenburg and Louis Meyer were two boys who attended. The first mixed-gender religious school class in 1893 was taught by a Mrs. Hattie Cohn and attended by Fay Netter, Clarence and Dan Scharff, Edgar and Hortence Herman, Clara Hirsch, Leo Ellenberg, Irving Levy, Jay Altschul, Dora and Hattie Weigle, and a lad named Ray M. We can see familiar names of both the Reform and Orthodox community.

The Sunday School originally was held in a church on the corner of Olive and Jefferson Streets, which has since been demolished. When the Woodruff Building opened in 1911, just next door, the religious school leadership seized the opportunity to rent a space.

In 1897, the religious school hired a rabbinical student from Hebrew Union College (HUC) by the name of Herman Rosenwasser to teach the students. In order to support himself, Herman also taught German, Greek, and Latin at the city's high school. Rosenwasser led the congregation in worship through the spring of 1903, before returning to the seminary to

Herman Rosenwasser *Courtsey Central High School, Springfield.*

complete his studies. HUC had been founded in Cincinnati, Ohio, in 1875 as the first Reform rabbinical seminary on the continent. Its faculty and student body were almost exclusively German-born immigrants, or their sons, and was very much involved in the Reform Movement. The dominance of German Jews was to be expected given that Eastern European Jews had not yet been Americanized. Herman was a typical HUC student, having been born in Austro-Hungary in 1878 and immigrated to the United States in 1898 after finishing school.

His background afforded him well in the teaching of German. After graduating from HUC in 1908, Herman eventually relocated to San Francisco where he worked as a rabbi and wrote the statement for the Scopes Monkey Trial about how the original Hebrew Bible was not in conflict with the theory of evolution. Herman's willingness to leave seminary in order to teach religious school may have been in response to the dearth of qualified religious schoolteachers at that time. The wealth of the Jewish community in Springfield at the time is attested to by the fact that they could afford a teacher. Most small communities could not and, thus, had to rely on uneducated and untrained volunteers.

At some point after the founding of Sha'are Zedek, their Ladies Aid Society began sponsoring the Religious School. In 1927, B'nai Brith, a men's charitable group, paid for the room used by the Religious School, rented from M. F. Smith. Near the end of 1928, the Sister-hood of Temple Israel, which had made numerous donations to the school over the years, was asked to join in the sponsorship. In 1930, the B'nai Brith announced they would take over the sponsorship of the Religious School, which offered instruction to almost 40 children under the tutelage of Mrs. J. Karchmer and three other teachers. By 1940, the Religious School teacher was being paid by the Sisterhood for his services. In 1941, there were 25 children in the Religious School divided into four classes. Two of the teachers were volunteers, while Edith Breadman and Mr. Simon were paid.

                 CREATING COMMUNITY

From left to right, Suzie Goerlick, Laura Arbeitman, Rabbi Ernst Jacob,
Steven Bass, Allene Fetter at the 1964 Confirmation ceremony.
Courtesy The History Museum on the Square.

Rabbi Karl Richter held the first Confirmation class in the early 1940s. The ceremony for Confirmation was instituted in the United States by Rabbi Max Lilianthal in the mid-1800s. Rabbi Isaac Mayer Wise, the founder of Hebrew Union College, believed that the Confirmation ceremony, which included girls and boys, "extended its [the synagogue's] benevolent influence over the daughters of Israel as well as the sons."[5] Held at *Shavuot*—the festival celebrating the receiving of the Ten Commandments—the process of Jewish Confirmation was modeled after the Christian catechism, providing Jewish youths with a rite of passage analogous to their Christian counterparts. Moreover, for girls it marked major event in the cycle of life that acknowledged their commitment to Judaism. Four students were confirmed on May 24, 1942.

During the 1941-1942 school year, there were only three teachers: Rabbi Richter, Miss Sussman, and Mr. Simon. The Orthodox community had no religious school, so many of the families, like Ben and Fannie Arbeitman, joined both congregations just so their children could get a religious education.

During the 1930s and 1940s, Nathan Karchmer served as a co-director of the religious school along with Lester Strauss and Fannie Arbeitman. Ms. Kramer, Molly Kransberg and Mrs. Jake Karchmer volunteered as teachers.

The next official Religious School report was given in 1970 by Manny Smith. Smith raised concerns that the school was shrinking, despite the fact that 39 children were enrolled in the school at the time of his report. Additionally, Rabbi David Wucher, the student rabbi, had reinstituted Confirmation. The teachers were Edna Arbeitman, Nadine Smith, and Gytel Lotven. In 1973, a new Sunday School Committee that included Fred Hamburg, Manny Smith, Jean Mace, and Darlene Rubenstein was formed to address the issue.

In 1980, Stefan Broidy was appointed as the Religious School Director with the assistance of Cindy Kraft (now Platz). The school had 40 students. In 1981, the enrollment had grown to 60 with an active youth group. By the next century, however, the community had shrunk, and the religious school declined to as few as ten students.

The rise and fall in numbers in the religious school reflects not only the peaks and valleys in the congregation membership, but also the flow of generations. Sociologists call this population cycles and it has to do with the economic stability of the family and community along with, in small communities, the emigration and immigration patterns.

Cemetery

The founding of a Jewish cemetery was, across the United States, a defining moment for a Jewish community, whose need to bury the dead in a sanctified place encouraged informal Jewish social circles to organize formally. The Jewish cemetery in Springfield was founded in 1893, with the internment of Ella Weigle, who had died of diphtheria. Previously, Jewish families either had their deceased kinspeople transported to St. Louis— where many families maintained relations—to be buried in one of that city's Jewish cemeteries, or Jewish families bought plots in the local Hazelwood Cemetery.

It was not until July 26, 1914, however, that a committee comprised of Charles Altschul, Moses Levy, and Max Scharff was appointed to create some by laws concerning who could be buried in the cemetery. In 1916, Isaac Glaser and Max Scharff were appointed to a new committee to study the matter. At its February 15, 1916 meeting, the board of directors of Temple Israel approved a policy that dictated "no resident of Springfield

The original entrance at Temple Israel Cemetery prior to the damage done 1920. *Courtesy Rosemary Rubenstein.*

not a member of this congregation shall have the privilege of buying a lot in our cemetery under any circumstance," while allowing impoverished Springfield Jews to petition for an exclusion from the need to purchase a lot.[6] Since at this time only Jews were members of the congregation, the policy effectively meant that the cemetery was exclusively reserved for Jewish internments. It seems the term congregation was meant to be as inclusive of the local Jewish community as possible because Orthodox Jews were also buried in the cemetery.

In 1985, the community instituted new cemetery guidelines permitting the internment of the spouses and children of "persons of the Jewish faith," following new policies in the congregation and the Reform Movement more broadly that granted non-Jews some form of membership in the synagogue.[7] In the 1970s, the Reform Movement came to recognize that a Jewish family did not require both parents to be Jewish. This national ruling changed the congregation's make-up, thereby creating a need to accommodate mixed-faith marriages

The original gates to the cemetery were damaged in 1920. The following year, the board requested the cemetery warden to have them repaired.

The cemetery was maintained not only through the selling of plots, but also through donations, such as the $25 gift that the Ladies Aid Society of Temple Israel gave in 1922. In 1925, the cemetery fund was formally separated from the synagogue fund.

In 1943, Joe Rubenstein donated the funds to erect a permanent wall around the cemetery in memory of his wife Rose. Because the cemetery abuts the Hazelwood and National Cemeteries (the latter being a cemetery for veterans), this wall was considered better than the wooden fence that had marked the holy space for the Jewish community. The board, in turn, promised to maintain the wall in perpetuity. In 2001, the old chat-covered road that had long served the cemetery was paved. In August 2015, Mark Ekhaus completed repairs to the wall that age had inflicted.

Houses of Worship

In 1893 the first public announcement of Jewish services in Springfield was published in the newspaper. The occasion was *Rosh Hashanah* and the services were held in the Christian Church on College Street, but there were not enough seats for everyone who wished to attend. Abe J. Messing, a rabbinical student, led the services for both *Rosh Hashanah* and *Yom Kippur* speaking on "Sincerity, Tolerance and More Light" and "Submission."[8] The Torah that was used was owned by Jake Marx and a choir sang. The following year he returned and spoke on "It is Soon Gone and We Fly Away" and one in the morning entitled "Atonement and At-one-ment."[9] High Holy Day services were often led by student rabbis from HUC. Then the community arranged to hold services in the sanctuary of the South Street Christian Church.

Shortly thereafter, the Jewish community began renting space at the Martin's Piano Store for worship. Martin's was located one block south of the square on Walnut Street to the east. In the 1910s, the congregation moved east across the street into the Chickering Piano Store, above which was home to the Masonic Lodge. The building had been built in 1906. Temple Israel advertised their Yom Kippur services in the 1916 newspaper. Jake Marx led the *Shabbat* (Sabbath) services and was joined by Dan Herman, Max Schwab, Dave Schwab, and Max Scharff on occasion. In its early history, the congregation would hire a student rabbi to lead the services during the High Holy Days. In 1909, Samuel S. Cohon was brought in to lead services; he later became a leader in the Reform Movement, guiding the creation of a prayer book and Haggadah and Reform theology. In 1923,

High Holy Day services were held in the First Presbyterian Church. There were about 20 families who belonged to the Reform congregation during the early 1900s.

The pattern of renting space in which to hold worship services dates back to the Colonial Period. After the founding of a community, Jewish congregants often rented space before endeavoring to construct their own building. Utilizing rental properties near downtown where Jewish businesses were generally located, as was the case in Springfield, was not uncommon. It was convenient and, while not done purposely, the concentration of their business activities tended to make the Jewish minority's presence seem more pronounced than it might actually have been. Moreover, the use of Christian houses of worship was also common and highlights the Christian community's acceptance of their Jewish neighbors. In 1899, there was discussion of Temple Israel buying the First Congregational Church property on the corner of Jefferson Avenue and Locust Street.

The First Building

The push for a building rather than renting a space began in earnest in 1924, when the board of directors of Temple Israel voted "that the president appoint a committee to buy a lot and build a temple."[10] There seems to have been little action taken, as no committee was appointed, until 1928 when Marx Netter, L. Nathan, Sol Wolf, Mrs. David Schwab, and Julia Rothschild were called upon "to look for better quarters to hold our services."[11] The group was reappointed to continue their work in October 1929.

In October 1929, Mrs. David Schwab, Mrs. Doggrell, Mrs. Fayman, and Miss Tess Levy hosted a dinner at Mrs. Schwab's home to kick-off fundraising for the project. Their efforts raised $49.30 for the cause. The Sisterhood committee of Mrs. Max Schwab, Mrs. Moe Fayman, Miss Tess Levy, Mrs. Netter, Mrs. Dave Schwab, Mrs. Strauss, and Mrs. Weil decided to pitch-in with their own fundraising event throwing a luncheon the following month. The push by the women of the congregation for a house of worship and the marshaling their energies on behalf of fundraising efforts was not unusual in the American Jewish experience. However, historian Hasia Diner finds it interesting that women, who traditionally had no power in the congregation, took such a strong stand on this issue and won. In 1930, Temple Israel built their first building on property owned by David and Max Schwab. The Jewish population in the city was approx imately 360,

The original South Street Christian Church. *Courtesy South Street Christian Church.*

only 0.63 percent of the Springfield's total population. The building cost $16,000, which, adjusted for inflation, would approach a quarter of a million dollars in 2020.

Rabbi H. A. Iola of Tulsa dedicated the building on November 30, 1930, while "two Christian ministers" also spoke at the event.[12] The inclusion of Christian ministers in the ceremony is significant, as it shows the importance to Reform congregations of tying religious and public life together, as well as the level of acceptance the Jewish community had gained in the city. The first tablet honoring donors to the congregation was presented by Mr. and Mrs. Joe Rubenstein. In 1933, the Sisterhood donated $500 to help pay the mortgage. They did so again in 1935, 1936, 1937, and 1938. In

The Chickering Piano Store on East Walnut Street and the Masonic Lodge next to the bent telegraph pole. *Courtesy The History Museum on the Square.*

The first building on the corner of Kickapoo Avenue and Belmont Street. *Courtesy The History Museum on the Square.*

1940, David Schwab announced that only $1000 was left on the mortgage. In 1944, Harry Rope and Ed Lurie paid off the remaining mortgage. In 1946, the Temple Israel Memorial Fund was created to specifically maintain the building.

Merging the Congregations

In 1946, the Orthodox Congregation joined Temple Israel because the Orthodox's numbers were shrinking. The expenses to rent their own space and hire a student rabbi were too much for the Orthodox community to bear.

The future monies and membership were merged, though any funds previously gathered were to remain dedicated to their specific uses. Temple Israel's by-laws were adopted. The congregation's name was changed to United Hebrew Congregations. The use of the plural was in recognition of the two communities that had chosen to work together. The membership list was to note each member as either Orthodox or Reform and the rabbi was to be ordained by a Reform seminary, according to the agreed upon by-laws. This continued until the 1980s. Despite consideration in 1976 to abolish the practice of labeling families with the designation, the membership voted against it. Use of the plural became problematic in later years, however, as it functioned to maintain division between the two communities of practice.

Rabbi H. A. Iola. *Courtesy Temple Israel, Tulsa, Oklahoma.*

In 1946, Ben Karchmer was appointed to lead the Orthodox services and Irving Schwab the Reform. By 1950, there were only 200 Jews in Springfield. Nonetheless, in the next three years, the membership grew by 50. By 1959, though there were just 210 Jews in the city, the congregations maintained separate services. The Friday service times were staggered: Reform at 8 P.M. and Orthodox at 7 P.M. or 7:30 P.M. As a result in some members attending both services. Irving Schwab was influential in getting the two congregations to merge. In 1953, the Orthodox membership petitioned the board of directors to make the rabbi conduct their services as well as for the creation

Temple Israel's theater group, the Center Players. Seated are Sylvia Goldberg,
Saul Goldberg, Lena Rosen, Betty Arbeitmen, and Ronnie Bisman.
In the back are Bob Bisman, David Kenton, and Ben S. Arbeitman.
Courtesy Special Collections and Archives, Missouri State University.

of a unified service. The board contacted Rabbi Haddox in Kansas City for
an example of a unified service.

Bernard Fetter, Ena Tarrasch, and Arthur Rosen polled the congregants
during the 1960s to discover what kind of services would suit the congregations and the results were then used to create an acceptable service for
both parties. Starting in 1950, there was a push among Reform congregations for more rituals, this probably eased the religious merging of the
two Springfield congregations. While the national trend was that Reform
congregations were attracting more traditional members at least in small
communities it was more a matter of them merging to survive.

The 1975 *Gates of Prayer: The New Union Prayer Book* was published
by the Central Conference of American Rabbis (CCAR) included more
Hebrew than in their previous prayerbook and a return to many of the traditional portions of the Jewish liturgy. In 1976, Rabbi Wucher decided to
study the new prayerbook to see if it would be appropriate for the Springfield
services. At the same time William "Bob" Karchmer asked Chaim Lotven

to purchase a number of these new prayerbooks in memory of his mother, hoping that the gesture would to give the congregation the opportunity to review the CCAR's revisions. Additionally, he was "concerned that the present books are in rather bad condition, are not being replaced, are not being repaired, and . . . are not any longer in print." He asked Jerry and Thelma Caplan to join him in the project. Eventually, Wucher decided that after the 1976 High Holy Days, the congregation would begin using the new prayerbooks. By this point, aided by the new prayerbook, the congregations joined services. However, the Orthodox congregation held their own High Holy Day services led by Nathan Karchmer, though the 1976 services were conducted by Dr. Isadore Fish of St. Louis in Nathan's absence.

Rabbi Uriel Smith convinced the shrinking Orthodox congregation in 1983 that the new Reform prayerbook was not that different from the Orthodox and the two congregations should pray together. Situated on the periphery of the Midwest and the South, the Springfield experience was typical as the merging of the two congregations—especially the folding of the Orthodox into the Reform, happened in just about every small town in the southern United States.

Expansion of the Building

The use of the synagogue as a community center became fairly common in small communities. This was the place where people socialized after prayer and a separate venue was often a financial burden to the community. Beginning in 1947, United Hebrew Congregations began considering a new building. By the middle of the year, this was changed to a new addition to the existing building. The idea began at a meeting in Mr. Sass' house where Isadore Lotven suggested that they should "build a community center— for everybody—every Jewish person" a plan originally suggested in 1939.[13] The use of the synagogue as a community center became fairly common in small communities. This was the place where people socialized after prayer and a separate venue was often a financial burden to the community. Mr. Manuel Morris of Kansas City was the architect and was paid $250 for his completed plans in April 1949. Immediately, a committee was organized to get bids for the construction and investigate buying existing homes for conversion. In 1950, the decision was made to build an addition that necessitated the raising of at least $25,000. The addition would have classrooms, a kitchen, and place for the Orthodox members to worship. When work began on the Community Center at the end of 1953, the estimated cost of the project was $50,000. This expansion was part of the trend among synagogues in the U.S. Not until December 7, 1953 when the addition, named the Jewish Community Center, was approved. On the request of Lena Rosen, a stage was added to the main hall of the Center in 1957.

In 1970, the Sisterhood requested permission to remodel the kitchen at a cost of approximately $5000. They were granted permission to remove walls and renovate. Beginning in 1995, the kitchen was officially declared to be considered "kosher style."[14] Therefore, pork and shellfish were not permitted, and meat and dairy could not be served together.

Desecration of the Synagogue

The members of the Jewish community as a whole has been reticent until recently to talk about antisemitism that they have confronted in Springfield, as they believed it only fueled the fire. Thus, the cross burning on the front yard of the synagogue on Belmont Avenue was forgotten except by a very few. In 1993, Fannie Arbeitman, who arrived in Springfield in 1935, would only say that it was "long ago."[15] Hal Lurie, son of Edward Lurie, who places the ugly episode in the 1930s, distinctly remembers the indignation of the locals at the time. No contemporaneous reference to the incident, however, is made in either of the local newspapers, nor in the minutes of the synagogue's board. A single reference does appear in the June 1948 minutes of B'nai Brith Lodge 717, in which it is noted that "Nathan Karchmer made report Anti defamation [*sic*] about the cross that was burned in front of Temple."[16] Isadore Lotven was very clear that "there was nothin' that you could do about it," though many of the local preachers were upset by it, the congregation "didn't make a big deal over it."[17]

In the 1950s and 1960s, there were numerous instances of swastikas painted on the exterior of the synagogue building. Simone Lovten Sofian, who was born and raised in Springfield, considers these to be responses to the local Jewish community's support of the Civil Rights Movement. This graffiti was never reported to the police. At least one of the incidents made the newspaper in which a non-Jewish journalist expressed outrage at the incident. There was also one incident in the 1980s that was reported to the police. Some members of the synagogue quietly debated if they should "leave it up for everyone to see or remove it and take away the pleasure of the perpetrators."[18] Rabbi Stuart Federow, who grew up in Springfield and lives in Houston, refers to this as Jewish Uncle Tomism, Jews who are "afraid to be outwardly, openly, proudly Jewish."[19] He notes that Jews are taught to be invisible or indistinguishable from the majority.

Despite the episodic expressions of antisemetism, it was not until 1989 that the local Jewish community became concerned enough to worry about security during services. The Springfield Police Department alerted the congregation to a rise of hate groups in the area and suggested that the congregation establish connections with the Neighborhood Watch Program. The board had the police department do a security review which returned a report that focused primary on prevention of property crime, such as adding locks, and installing security glass and stronger doors. After the murders of a number of Jews in Los Angeles, the congregation increasingly felt their security was compromised. Thus, they investigated hiring off-duty law enforcement officers to work as security guards during the High Holy Days. The use of security continued until 2005, when the practice was discontinued because it was determined that "a uniformed officer becomes a target."[20] Instead, a member of the congregation who serves as a police officer volunteered to do undercover work.

The Second Building

In 1986, the board of directors first "consider[ed] the possibilities of selling the current facility and purchasing a new one" and Jolyn Arbeitman was made chair of that committee.[21] They also considered constructing a new building. One site considered was property owned by United Hebrew Congregations next to the cemetery. In 1987, the Future Planning Committee listed a new building as their number one priority.

In 1988, the congregation was surveyed, and this showed that the congregation felt if there was extra revenue, the congregation preferred it be spent on a new building with renovation of the current one not far behind. The Future Planning Committee reported that the biggest hindrances to moving to a new building was lack of money to buy a property and no interest by a buyer in the current one.

At the 1989 annual meeting, the Building Committee announced the Mildred LeBolt Capital Endowment Fund should be committed to either renovation or new construction. They cautioned that "as our building ages, we can expect maintenance costs to increase and major expenses to develop," but because of zoning restrictions selling their building would be difficult.[22]

Starting in 1993, the congregation made plans to move. Jake Lotven, whose father helped found Sha'are Zedek, purchased the land for the new building and planted the courtyard in memory of his wife Sophie.

Bids for construction arrived in 1994 and 1995, but in 1995 President Joel Persky announced that "we've hit a major snag . . . the cost . . . for the Temple is $133,000 higher than the original estimates" and, therefore, the project had to be re-evaluated. The building had to be made more modest and "the ground breaking ceremony has been indefinitely postponed."[23] The groundbreaking for the building was on a cold January 21, 1996. The first services held in the building were in September of that year for *Rosh Hashanah*. Caleb Kraft had the first bar mitzvah in the building in early October 1996 and later that month his mother Cindy married John Platz in the first wedding ceremony in the new building.

Women's Role in the Congregations

Orthodox communities traditionally kept the genders separated during services either using the aisle down the center of the room as a divider or putting the women in a balcony. However, the Orthodox congregation in Springfield ended the segregation of genders during services. However, when the congregations joined, the one vote per household at congregational meetings was maintained until the 1970s, as the constitution read: "that the family member (family included wife, sons until twenty-one, and daughters until married) may not vote."[24] This was a fairly standard practice in American Reform congregations, and the restriction would not change until the 1970s. This, however, did not stop women from serving on the board. The first, Mrs. Julia Rothschild, was elected in 1925. In 1946, the president of the Sisterhood was added to the synagogue's board of directors.

In June of 1970 Bob Bisman reported to the board that "there has been some pressure in allowing an additional vote for the wives." This was not voted upon because of "some lengthy discussion."[25] The Sisterhood again

Temple Israel's second building located in Rogersville.
Courtesy Telling Traditions Project.

requested a review of the unresolved voting issue in 1972. President Hal Lurie declared he would investigate the by-laws "and meet with the concerned females."[26] The Sisterhood petitioned the board again in February 1973. Their requests included that there be one membership vote per couple and any congregation member should be eligible to sit on the board. Bill Karchmer, chair of the Constitution & By-laws Committee, was assigned the task of reviewing these requests. The issue had not yet been resolved by the middle of 1975, when Bernard Fetter reminded the board about it. A committee of Bob Kramer, George Rubenstein, Stanley Levitch, Herschal Kramer, and Mark Rosen was appointed to make changes to the Constitution and By-laws regarding the matter.

The congregation was polled and agreed that the by-laws regarding voting privileges needed to be revised. In the 1976 revision of the Constitution and By-laws rules were changed to stipulate that "each spouse may cast one-half vote, provided each spouse qualified for membership" and "that any regular member and his or her spouse may hold office."[27] It was not until 1989 that the first woman, Vicki Burstin, was voted in as president of the congregation.

Choir

The first mention of singers joining Temple Israel services appear in the October 9, 1921 board minutes in which it approved a resolution to pay Mrs. Lewis and Mrs. Huppner, and, when available, Mrs. Huppner's daughter, to sing for the congregation. None of these women were members of Temple Israel.

In 1923, the board of directors decided they wanted a "quire [*sic*] for Friday night services" and Moses Levy was put in charge of organizing one.[28] Mrs. Lewis was paid for her services in the choir yet again. However, organizing a choir from among the congregants was the real aim. In 1927, Max Scharff and Burton Freiberg were put in charge of this endeavor.

No mention further mention of any type of choir is made until the October 1971 board meeting, though the Reform congregation continued to hire a Christian choir to sing during the High Holy Day services. A number of the

Vicki Burstin in 1994.
Courtesy Temple Israel, Springfield.

The Temple Israel Choir, including Ken Burstin, Mara W. Cohen Ioannides,
Bobbie Kallembach, Judith Peavey, Linda Skolnik, Julia Watts Belser,
Elizabeth Weiner, and June Weiss, among others. *Courtesy the author.*

Orthodox Jews, however, objected to Christians singing religious music during services. It is also mentioned noted that during the

Mr. Millenhoff played piano and sang during services when the rabbi was not in attendance. Because a *minyan* (the ten required adults to conduct services) could not be organized, Isadore Lotven suggested that they only be hired when the rabbi was in attendance.

In 1973, the Religious Service Committee, consisting of Jerome Caplan, George Rubenstein, Martin Goldenberg, and David LeBolt, recommended that only a vocalist, rather than a choir, be used during services. At the end of 1973, Ernest Tarrasch resigned as music director and organist for Temple Israel, partially, as he told the Board, "due to his frustration at not being able to find a permanent reliable soloist."[29] He agreed to conduct the music for the High Holidays in 1974, where he would be joined by Ruth Palmer as the vocalist. However, someone else would have to sing and play the organ the rest of the year. Ernest continued in this revised role for a number of years.

For many years a fee of $15 per service was paid to each singer employed. Mr. and Mrs. Snook offered, in 1985, to sing for $25 per service, but because of the synagogue's financial problems, the board recommended that they only be employed every other Friday.

In 1987, the Youth Group offered to act as a choir, which does not appear to have been acted upon. A 1988 congregational survey shows that ten percent of the congregation suggested the choir be eliminated to save money. This was the number one suggestion. Ten percent also suggested a congregational choir, while four percent suggested the choir be eliminated entirely. Ernest Tarrasch had become ill in 1988, causing concern about his ability to return as the congregational organist.

The High Holy Days of 1989 were the first in which neither a choir nor an organist accompanied the service. At the year, however, Rabbi Bruce Diamond strongly suggested the creation of a congregational choir. Stefan Broidy and Kenneth Burstin headed up the effort as they began organizing a choir filled entirely with volunteers who were not required to audition, or read music or Hebrew. The newly formed choir would sing for the Jewish holidays and special events.

When Stefan retired from Missouri State University (MSU) and moved away, Ken became the sole choir director and Mark Rushefsky became the accompanist. The choir not only had the opportunity to sing with Jewish musicians as back-up, but also supported the Jewish congregation in Joplin as they sang during a Friday night service in the aftermath of the disastrous 2011 tornado.

Rabbi Karl Richter

As the Nazis gained more and more power, Jews worked to flee Germany and come to the United States. However, the American government had issued quotas on Jewish immigrants. One way around those quotas was for a refugee to have guaranteed employment. Thus, in the late 1930s, small congregations all over the country found a way to support rabbis, Temple Israel included.

The push for a German rabbi was begun by Minnie Hirsch in 1938. In December of that year, attorney and congregation member Irving Schwab wrote the young senator from Missouri, Harry S. Truman, "respectfully request[ing] you to render whatever assistance you can give toward" getting Rabbi Karl Richter a visa.[30] The congregation promised a two-year contract and annual salary of $1, 500, which would require a "substantial" dues increase for members and the Sisterhood would contribute an additional $25 to his monthly salary, but "this congregation [was] most desirous

Rabbi Karl Richter.
Courtesy Richter Family.

of obtaining Rabbi Richter for it has no religious leader in this City [*sic*] at all."[31]

On January 4, 1939 Senator Truman sent a letter to Samuel W. Honaker, the American Consul General, in support of the rabbi's visa. On May 17, 1939 Karl and Ruth Richter and their three-year-old daughter Esther arrived in the United States. Having already survived Kristallnacht and a Nazi round up of men in the congregation he was serving in Mannheim, Germany, he agreed with his wife to flee the country. Even though he felt guilt at leaving his congregation and family, he "knew the game was lost" and, as he explained to a reporter in Tampa, Florida, he drew solace from the line in Deuteronomy: "Choose life, that you and your children may life."[32] Ruth had lied in a cable to the congregation and stated that her husband's English was "perfect," when in fact Karl had originally written it was not good, but he was a "fast learner."[33]

It was in 1941 with Karl's suggestion that the congregation began using the newly revised Union Prayer Book and the congregation purchased its first shofar. He also once led services for the Orthodox congregation and conducted services at the Federal Medical Center. Additionally, Fort Leonard Wood, about one hundred miles northeast of Springfield, invited Rabbi Richter to lead services. Richter also instituted tours of the synagogue for non-Jewish groups as a way of educating them about Judaism. He did four of these in 1942.

As part of the rabbi's work in outreach in 1941, he informed the Board that he gave "51 addresses before non-Jewish organizations, civic clubs, churches, . . . schools and colleges" with 12 being outside of Springfield.[34] In 1942, he spoke to 32 Springfield organizations and five outside of Springfield. This kind of work was common in small Jewish communities as Reform congregations hoped to make a positive public image.

The family stayed in Springfield until 1942, when Karl took a position in Sioux Falls, South Dakota. The entire family is grateful to Temple Israel because the community saved them.

Rabbi Ernest Israel Jacob

In 1943, Rabbi Ernest I. Jacob, a seventeenth-generation rabbi, was hired as the rabbi for Temple Israel. He and his family were also Holocaust refugees. In 1938, he was taken from Augsberg, Germany, where he was the rabbi, and sent to Dachau for a month with 150 men from his congregation. His release was contingent on his leaving Germany immediately. He, his wife, and two sons left for England with only 10 marks and what personal items they could carry. There his sister took them in. It was there that Ernest perfected his English, though he never lost his German accent.

After a year in England, Mrs. Annette Jacob's family in St. Joseph arranged for Ernest to serve as a principal of a Hebrew school. In 1943, the family moved to Springfield where Ernest served both the Orthodox and Reform congregations. The reason this was possible was because Ernest found his Liberal Jewish upbringing to be at times more traditional than the Orthodox of Springfield. In fact, his house was for a time one of the two strictly kosher homes in the city; the other being that of Jenny Lotven. When his son Walter went to rabbinical seminary, Walter would return to Springfield during his breaks and would lead the Orthodox services and his father, the rabbi, the Reform.

Rabbi Jacob may have been the first rabbi in Springfield willing to take the pulpit at both the Reform and Orthodox

Rabbi Ernest Jacob.
Courtesy Springfield News-Leader.

congregations, but it was not the first time the community had attempted such an agreement. In 1917, upon the advice of Rabbi Bernard Cantor of Wichita, Kansas, the two congregations raised several thousand dollars to secure a rabbi that would serve both communities. This did not come to fruition, however. This could be because of the First World War where money and energy were devoted to more immediate issues, or that an agreeable candidate could not be found.

With a degree in Oriental languages and rabbinic ordination, Rabbi Jacob taught Hebrew Bible and history at Drury University. He expanded his rabbinic work to include O'Reilly Hospital and when that closed at the end of World War II, the Federal Medical Center. Additionally, he worked with the Rotary Club, University Club, Community Chest, B'nai Brith, the Springfield Ministerial Alliance, and the State's Human Rights Commission. He regularly worked with the American Legion speaking to them during their "Back to G-d" rallies and leading their parades. Ernest spoke to just about any group, if asked. For example, in 1950, he spoke to the Wesley Foundation of Missouri State University and in 1954 led the First Congregational Church for one Sunday when they were without a religious leader. It was not unusual for him to speak to three different groups in one week, often giving tours to Christian groups of the synagogue.

He presided over the consolidation of Temple Israel and Sha'are Zedek into United Hebrew Congregations in 1946. The merging of the two congregations had little to do with theological issues and much to do with practical ones. Many of the communal groups had members from both the Orthodox and Reform congregations, like B'nai Brith and the Sisterhood. The idea was first presented by Irving Schwab and the ultimate end was because of Rabbi Jacob's diplomatic talents. The two groups shared a building but maintained separate services. In fact, the building was expanded in 1954 to include a chapel for Orthodox services. Their first president was Edgar Herman.

In 1964, the Jacobs retired. In 1969, they moved to Pittsburgh, Pennsylvania where their son Walter was rabbi at one of the largest synagogues in the country—Rodeph Shalom. In 1974, they died together of carbon monoxide poisoning in their Pittsburgh home. Ernest was so beloved that in 2013 "the portion of U.S. Highway 160 in Greene County from the intersection of West Mount Vernon Street to one-half mile south of . . . West Sunshine Street" was named "Rabbi Ernest I. Jacob Memorial Highway."[35]

Inter-Rabbi Years

When the congregations had no rabbi, congregation members like Arthur Rosen stepped in and lead services and the congregation hired student rabbis to come once a month. Nathan Karchmer requested that "one of the men in the Congregation takes over the Friday night services when no rabbi was available."[36]

Rabbi Uriel Smith

The next rabbi was Uriel Smith. Born in the United Kingdom, he lived in Israel between 1949 and 1956, before he was ordained at HUC in 1969. Smith was hired in 1972, when United Hebrew Congregations was unable to hire their student rabbi David Wucher full-time as he had opted to enter the Chaplaincy for the Armed Forces. Uriel was installed on August 23, 1972, by Rabbi Alvin Rubin of Temple Israel in St. Louis. Mrs. Saul Goldberg, Sisterhood president, blessed the candles, Jerome Caplan blessed the Torah before its reading, and Robert Kramer after. Ernest Tarrasch was the musical director and the Sisterhood sponsored the *oneg* (after services social). Along with his rabbinical position, Smith taught Hebrew Bible and biblical history at MSU and served as the Jewish chaplain at the Federal Medical Center for Federal Prisoners. He resigned

Rabbi Uriel Smith.
Courtesy Temple Israel, Springfield

on July 30, 1975. He is remembered by Temple Israel members as an earnest rabbi and with "gentle spirit."[37] Gerrit tenZythoff, former head of the Religious Studies Department at MSU, called him "a truly profound teacher and marvelous colleague."[38]

Rabbi David Wucher

Rabbi David Wucher was first a student rabbi for the congregation between 1969 and 1972. It was during this time that the *bat mitzvah* ceremony was introduced. The *bat mitzvah*, meaning daughter of the commandments, was first performed in 1922 by Judith Kaplan, daughter of Rabbi Mordecai Kaplan. It did not become popular until the 1960s, however, and the Orthodox Movement has only instituted a *bat mitzvah* ceremony in the last decade. Wucher was hired in 1975 as a full-time rabbi beginning with the High Holy Days services and stayed until 1978 when he left to pursue a doctorate in Jewish History. After completing his degree, he returned to being a congregational rabbi, though not in Springfield. During his tenure with United Hebrew Congregations, Wucher taught at MSU and confirmed Ruth Rubenstein and Bernard Kramer. Upon leaving his position at Temple Israel, he and his family were given an indefinite honorary membership.

Rabbi Solomon Kaplan

Rabbi Solomon Kaplan, the former director of the Southwest Region of the Union of American Hebrew Congregations, was hired in 1979. He was a lover of children having helped found the Henry S. Jacobs Camp in Mississippi where he served as its first director. At United Hebrew Congregations, he encouraged children to participate in the rituals. As was the case with his predecessor, Kaplan taught Hebrew Bible at MSU. When he opened the Sabbath services to visitors, Sol received resistance from some congregants. They felt they were being put "on parade," but the rabbi believed this would break down barriers with the

Rabbi Solomon Kaplan.
Courtesy Springfield News-Leader.

Christian community and create acceptance."[39] With this in mind, Rabbi Sol, Arthur Rosen, and Dianna Long formed *Or L'goyim* (Light to the World) in 1978. It was a group that provided information about Judaism to non-Jews. By March 1980, they had been interviewed on television, brought a dozen groups to the synagogue, and visited 36 others. When the Springfield Council of Churches (CC) broke with the Moral Majority, Sol decided it was time to create a rapport with them. Established in 1969, the CC's purpose "was . . . to unite people of the faith to improve the quality of life in the Springfield/Ozarks area," something to which he was dedicated.[40] However, neither he nor any rabbi following him were permitted to become a full member of the council board because the group does their work explicitly "in the name of Jesus Christ."[41] In 1981, Sol did 60 speaking engagements across Springfield and beyond. At this time, there were 94 member families. Despite the largest congregation ever, the group was insolvent and a Special Meeting of the congregants was called in May 1982 to brainstorm ideas to raise money. Teresa Tarrasch was appointed chair of a Ways and Means Com mittee. As a result of the committee's work, dues relief was granted by the United American Hebrew Congregations and an auction was organized that netted over $3,000.

Rabbi David Jeremy Zucker

Rabbi Kaplan died suddenly in 1983. Rabbi David Jeremy Zucker was not hired to replace him until 1984. In the interim, Stefan Broidy and Ken Burstin took turns leading services. Zucker had previously been in Birmingham, Alabama and had received both ordination and a doctorate. He primarily led the Reform services but would assist with the Orthodox worship when called upon. One of his innovations was to conduct services directed specifically towards children.

With the strong support of Chaim Lotven, an Orthodox congregant, and Paula Kaplan, Rabbi Kaplan's widow, Zucker also brought the Orthodox and Reform congregations together for joint High Holy Day services. He accomplished the feat by including more Hebrew in the liturgy than Reform Jews typically used. This was also possible with the new *Gates of Repentance Prayer Book* produced by the UAHC. The board mandated its use for the 1985 High Holy Day services.

Also during Zucker's tenure, the first interfaith Holocaust commemoration service was held on April 3, 1985, at South Street Christian Church. With the changes Zucker oversaw, the membership grew to 103 house

Rabbi David Zucker.
Courtesy Springfield News-Leader.

holds, rising 10 percent from the previous year. However, in 1986 the membership dropped to 91 dues-paying members. In addition to his work at United Hebrew Congregations, David taught at MSU and Drury University.

In 1987, Rabbi David Zucker's home was vandalized. A swastika was painted on the siding. The Council of Churches was "shocked and greatly saddened that such an action could happen in Springfield, Missouri."[42] As a gesture of support, they covered the deductible on the insurance policy so that David could repair the damage at no cost to himself. Jim Moyer, then, the head of the Religious Studies Department at MSU, also sent a letter of support to David. Outrage and disappointment were expressed both by the public and the editorial staff in the local newspaper. In the end, the incident was considered a disagreement between one of David's sons and a schoolmate. Ultimately, his contract was not renewed after 1988, because the congregational board did not feel he was a good match for the congregation.

Rabbi Bruce Diamond

Rabbi Bruce Diamond's tenure at United Hebrew Congregations lasted barely two years. His contract began August 1, 1989. As part of the continuing effort to work with the CC, the rabbi supported the council's request that the synagogue be open for tours and the board concurred. Additionally, he worked part-time at the Federal Medical Center for Federal Prisoners serving their Jewish inmates. In 1991, Diamond confessed that he and United Hebrew Congregations were not a good fit, expressing his desire to return to the East and his family.

Rabbi Rita Sherwin

In 1992, United Hebrew Congregations hired its first woman rabbi—Rita Sherwin. For her it was the fulfillment of "a childhood fantasy."[43] While traditionally Orthodox Jews do not accept women as rabbis, the Orthodox members were "completely supportive and accepting" of her as their rabbi. Members of the Reform community "admired" her.[44] For a number of years, she taught "Introduction to Judaism" in the Religious Studies Department at MSU, which was partially funded by the Jewish Chautauqua Association. She also coordinated Springfield's recognition of World AIDS Day in 1999, and joined the College of Clergy, which was "formed to look into issues affecting Springfield."[45] In 2005, Rita received an award from the AIDS Project of the Ozarks for her service. Additionally, she was a member of the Springfield Rotary Club, the Interfaith AIDS Network, and worked with the Jewish inmates at the Federal Medical Center.

During her time at United Hebrew Congregations, membership hit a high of 123 families. In 2007, Rita performed the first homosexual wedding ceremony in the city recognizing the relationship between two women in the congregation. The Reform Movement had supported

Rabbi Rita Sherwin.
Courtesy Telling Traditions Project

Rabbi Sherwin officiating the wedding of Billie Marsala and Anisa Dawn in 2007.
Photo by Robert Anderson, III. *Courtesy Billie Marsala and Anisa Dawn.*

homosexual civil marriages beginning in 1996, and 2000 they came out in "support . . . of those who choose to officiate at rituals of union for same-gender couples."[46]

One of her goals was to help create harmony among the different religious groups in Springfield. To make this happen, she helped found the Interfaith Alliance of the Ozarks and participated in Springfield Faith Voices, a group of the religious congregations advocating for social justice. Rabbi Rita worked on the Interfaith Thanksgiving Service and published essays in the local paper. As part of her interfaith efforts, she continued the relationship with the CC that Rabbi Kaplan had begun. In 1995, the congregation received a certificate of appreciation "for being such a good friend to the Council of Churches of the Ozarks and its projects."[47]

The impact that Rita had on the Springfield community was so profound that upon her retirement Mayor Robert L. Stephens proclaimed May 10, 2014 as Rabbi Rita Sherwin Day.

Conclusion

The current Jewish community of Springfield reflects many of the trends that have affected Jewish communities across the country, especially small ones. It began with a Reform congregation and later an Orthodox congregation was started. The two merged because it was impossible to maintain two separate congregations. There were student rabbis and, later, full-time rabbis. When women began to be ordained, their impact was felt in Springfield as the community embraced the change and hired a transformative leader. What makes this community different from most small communities is that it has persisted through the many changes that has marked its history. The larger trend has seen families send their children away to college only to lose those same children to presumably better opportunities elsewhere. Inasmuch as the young never return, the result is that many communities have aged to ultimately die away. However, with the growing economy and multiple institutes of higher education and hospitals, Temple Israel has been lucky enough to stay alive.

CHAPTER V

Charity and Community Service

CHARITY, ALSO KNOWN AS *tzaddakah* (the Hebrew word for justice or righteousness), and community service are basic tenants of Judaism. Thus, Jews joined local community organizations and formed their own to help fellow Jewish residents in need. Traditionally, Jewish law dictates that Jews have a responsibility to give to charity. Indeed, both Deuteronomy 26:12 and Leviticus 19 tell Jews how much of their income is to be given to the poor. In Europe, because Jews were not included as part of their local communities, they became semi-autonomous and developed their own communal system to provide for the sick, the ill, the widow, the orphan, and the dead. In the New World, this work was transferred from the management of a community board in Eastern Europe to charitable groups in the New World. With the growth of the funeral industry during the Civil War and separation of the dead from the living during the Victorian period, the caring of the dead moved from the home to the funeral home. Thus, the Jewish funeral societies moved from the caring of the dead to the caring of those left behind. Most of the Jewish charity took the form of caring for the ill, poor, and orphaned.

Springfield Ladies Saturday Club

The Springfield Ladies Saturday Club is the oldest club in the city, almost the first in the state, having been incorporated in 1894, although it was founded in 1878. The founding of Drury College in 1873 is believed to have given a push for the creation of this educational and charity group. Their educational goal was achieved by providing lectures to their members on divergent topics. Their hope was to "cultivate all things womanly, all things noble, all things pure."[1] Many of the founding members were former schoolteachers, including Mrs. Victor (Bertha) Sommers. Bertha does not appear on the membership rolls any time after the club's founding. It may be that the annual dues of $1 became difficult for Bertha when her husband's business failed.

Jewish Ladies Aid Society

The Ladies Aid Society, the women's philanthropic group associated with Temple Israel, was first listed in the *Jewish American Year Book* in 1914. The first mention appears in the Temple Israel board minutes for September 24, 1922, when the board thanked the group for a donation to the cemetery fund. The upkeep of the cemetery is a communal responsibility and Jewish women's benevolent societies often took care of the ill and dying, even preparing the dead for burial. Before the two Jewish congregations in the city merged, the Eastern European Jewish women were not warmly welcomed into the Ladies Aid Society. They, in fact, had organized their own benevolent society.

The Ladies Aid Society changed its name to the Sister-hood of Temple Israel on October 10, 1924, because they wanted to do more than just provide succor for the needy. It was not until the November 4, 1926, meeting of the society that the decision was made that every meeting be opened with a prayer. The Sister-hood provided charity to such groups as the Greene County Health Association, Travelers Aid, and Children's Home. A favorite charity was the Welfare House, which received regular donations from the Sister-hood throughout the years. Race presented no barrier to its philanthropic work, as the organization "contribute[d] to the support of a very needy colored family" in 1926.[2] In addition, the group made regular donations to the religious school for materials they needed. After the construction of the synagogue in 1930, the Sisterhood, according to board minutes, decided to "hold its business meetings in the Temple Assembly room and [continue to] serve refreshments," rather than conduct meetings in people's homes.[3] However, the social events would be held in homes or the assembly room depending upon the wishes of the hostess. The group continued its charity and social work for decades. It ran the gift shop during the 1990s, subsidized the Religious School, provided funds to Ozarks Food Harvest, hosted the annual *Yom Kippur* break-the-fast meal, kept the kitchen supplied, and paid for the cleaning of the building.

For a short time in the 1990s, the Sisterhood was reworked its mission to focus less on charity and more on self-education, and was redubbed Women of Valor. For a short time, there was still a Sisterhood that continued doing charity work. In 2001, with interest in belonging to the national organization waning, the Sisterhood officially withdrew its membership. Shortly thereafter it collapsed from disinterest but was revived in 2006, when the women in the congregation sought to create more social interaction and a forum for charitable works.

Masons and Other Societies

The Masons in Springfield are almost as old as the community itself. In 1841, the founding of the Ozark Lodge was approved by the Grand Lodge. In 1868, the lodges in Springfield merged and became the Solomon Lodge 271. In 1906, the Masons constructed a building on the corner of Walnut and Pearl Streets. Fraternal orders, like the Masons and the Odd Fellows, had reached their zenith in popularity in the late nineteenth century, as they met many middle-class and working-class men's need for sociability and a sense of personal and collective importance in midst of rapid industrialization and urbanization. Orders often provided a social safety net, offering members accident and sickness insurance, life insurance, and funerary services. Joining the Masons, and other societies, helped merchants establish connections in their communities. Thus, Jewish businessmen, such as Joseph Rubenstein and Moses Levy, recognized the value of participating in fraternal organizations. Because Masons believe in the omnipotent being, but follow no specific religion, any Jew could comfortably join. Indeed, Moses Levy was a member of the Masons from 1878 until his death in 1928. During the 1910s, Ben Moskowitz joined the local lodge. When he returned to Springfield after serving in World War I, he sat on the committee that oversaw the construction of the Abou Ben Adhem Shrine Mosque. First conceived in 1906, the building was to be the home to the newly founded Shriners. At a cost of $600,000, the structure was the largest auditorium west of the Mississippi upon its completion in 1923.

Later in the 20th century, Walter Rosenbaum, the child of Holocaust refugees, and his brother Sid both joined the Joplin Missouri Scottish Rites

Solomon Lodge 271 member, Ben Moskowitz, circa 1906. *Courtesy Mary Moskowitz Watters and Jim Watters.*

Masons. Walter received the rank of Master in 1993 and believes himself the first Jew locally to achieve such a rank.

Julius Cohn was a charter member and the treasurer of the North Springfield Lodge of the International Order of Odd Fellows. This group was officially chartered in 1870, coinciding with the founding of North Springfield. By 1883, the lodge had grown to 40 members. There seems to have been no other Jewish members of the Odd Fellows. Despite the relative inclusivity of the Odd Fellows, it is likely the more traditional institutions tethered to family and the synagogue offered sufficient social and charitable support and may have made membership in secular organizations appear redundant.

Jake Marx was an officer for the Knights of Honor in 1881. The Knights of Honor was, according to their rules, really a life insurance group for "all acceptable white men and women of any reputable profession, business, or occupation who are over eighteen and under fifty years of age."[4] They provided educational lectures to members and charity to the community. They were founded in 1873 by former members of the Ancient Order of United Workmen and the Independent Order of the Odd Fellows.

At the end of the nineteenth century, Charles Altschul and George Weigle had become members of the Elks and Knights of Pythias. Both a charitable and social group, the Elks were founded in New York in 1866, after the closure of saloons and theaters on Sundays. The Knights of Pythias was founded near the end of the Civil War in 1864, in Washington, D.C. as another charitable fraternity. Knights of Pythias' first lodge in Springfield was established nine years later. The fraternal order became so popular that the city was home to three lodges by 1883.

American Legion

When he died at the age of forty in 1930, the local press reported that Ben Moskowitz was "one of the oldest members of the American Legion in [the] city."[5] He belonged to Post 69, the only post in the city at the time. It was chartered August 1, 1920, less than a year after the American Legion had been chartered by Congress. One of the first accomplishments of the national organization was its advocacy for the creation of the United States Veterans Bureau that worked to get medical benefits for veterans. The bureau was later consolidated with other federal veteran programs under the Hoover administration to become the Veterans Administration. While not all Jewish veterans joined the organization, by 1931, there were eighteen other Jewish veterans who had become American Legion members: Maurice Barth (co-owner of Barth's on the Square), Edgar Herman (of Herman the Tailor), Jake Karchmer (of Karchmer Iron and Metal), Ben Lipman (the grocer), Arthur Marx (of The Marx Store), Arthur Rubenstein and Hershel Rubenstein (of Rubenstein's), and Irving Schwab (an attorney).

In 1931 or 1932, there are conflicting documents, Jake Karchmer organized the Last Man's Club, gathering World War I veterans to celebrate having survived the war and honor their dead comrades. In 1933, the

Scottish Rite Masons, Walter Sidney "Sid" Rosenbaum and Lother "Larry" Rosenbaum. *Courtesy Sid Rosenbaum.*

club had a total of 884 members, including the Jewish veterans listed above. Jake Karchmer was Commander of the Post in 1933. The following year, he was awarded a dollar for winning the club's annual storytelling contest. He became the Admiral of the Last Man's Club in 1940.

The last Jewish member of the club was Hershel Rubenstein who died in 1971. In 1992, the last surviving member of the club, V. Homer Wilson, received the bottle of champagne that the original members had purchased. Wilson was to drink a toast to his departed comrades.

B'nai Brith

Henry Jones, a German Jewish immigrant, had established B'nai Brith in 1843, as a philanthropic organization. The Springfield B'nai Brith Lodge No. 717, with its 29 founding members, was formally approved for affiliation with national body at the April 9, 1912 annual meeting of the District Grand

Lodge. The first lodge secretary in Springfield was Aubrey M. Ullman, and Solomon Wolf attended the district meeting to represent the Springfield chapter. At the end of 1912, there was $143.25 in the lodge account, and, though, the organization had a charitable mission, this did not preclude a social function, as a portion of the lodge funds were allocated to suppling members with cigars during the meetings. Both Reform and Orthodox men were eligible to join, so that by the middle of 1913, the lodge membership had grown to 35. In 1924, the lodge initiated 15 candidates including Ben Arbeitman, David LeBolt, Sidney Kemp, Isadore Lotven, Harry Fetter, Harry Simons, Ben Moskowitz, Ben Sussman, and Gus Marx. Their initiations proved to be a boon for the lodge's fundraising efforts as the meeting netted $1600 in pledges for the B'nai Brith Sanatorium slated to be built in Denver, Colorado.

In 1914, the lodge began subletting the space Temple Israel was using in the Masonic Lodge above the Chickering Piano Store. Beginning in 1923, it sublet from Sha'are Zedek, the Orthodox Jewish congregation, in the same building. Beginning in 1931, B'nai Brith paid $5 per month to hold their meetings in the Temple Israel Assembly Room. However, by 1935,

Springfield B'nai Brith Lodge No. 717 members, left to right Ben Arbeitman, Jake Lotven, Larry Rosenbaum, Isadore Lotven, Bill Arbeitman, Chaim Lotven, Leo Forbestein, and Rabbi David Wucher. *Courtesy Sid Rosenbaum.*

the meetings had been moved to the Kentwood Arms Hotel. Subsquent meetings were moved around town to the Green Tavern, the Moran Hotel, Heer's Tea Room, and the Colonial Hotel. At one point, members assembled at the Sorosis Club, but the arrangement did not last long because poker was forbidden there. This constant moving was tied to a desire to find affordable space. An agreement was finally made with United Hebrew Congregations that B'nai Brith would pay $200 a year for use of the building. In 1972, due to financial difficulties, the lodge was granted free use of the building. In 1979, the relief was rescinded, and B'nai Brith was charged $20 per month for the privilege.

One of the regular charitable works of the B'nai Brith was helping the sick in need. The organization often contributed to community funds and donated regularly to the Leo N. Levi Memorial Hospital in Hot Springs, Arkansas. Beginning in 1933, after hearing a lecture from Mr. Kaufman from a New York lodge, the lodge began a collection to help the Jews in Germany. They also supported the American Red Cross and the Colored United Services Organizations (USO).

In 1931, Nathan Karchmer and Arthur Rubenstein were tasked by the B'nai Brith with ensuring that "all Jews in our City have there [sic] papers showing them Citizens of the United States."[6] This committee was, at times, known as the Naturalization Committee and the Americanization Committee. In 1940, Hershel Rubenstein and Lester Strauss were appointed as the new committee and granted permission to work with the American Legion on the project. As this was during the rise of anti-Communist feelings in the United States, a growing antisemitic sentiment, and push against foreigners, especially Germans, this drive to prove American patriotism seems logical. Many Jews of Russian background joined the American Communist Party and, thus, the general population believed this association applied to all Jews. Thus, the desire to prove citizenship among the local Jewish population was a way to offset the anti-Communist push among American nationals.

Concerned by local, national, and especially international attitudes, a Public Relations committee was organized. Irving Schwab, J. H. Karchmer, Sam Stone, Ben Karchmer and M. Sass were to act as liaisons between the Lodge No. 771 and local churches, inviting local ministers to lecture at the synagogue. The first such lecture was given by Rev. Seckler on Friday, April 13, 1934.

For a short time, there was also a women's auxiliary of B'nai Brith in Springfield. Now known as Jewish Women International, B'nai Brith Women was officially established in San Francisco, California in 1909, and realized significant growth in the years preceding World War I. The organization arose at a time when women were emerging from the private sphere of the home to occupy a more visible position in the public sphere. During the war, B'nai Brith Women fulfilled their patriotic duties by rolling bandages, nursing wounded soldiers, and providing hospitality to servicemen far from home. The Springfield chapter was not organized until 1937. Its 14 members hosted a dance for the local community and assisted in hosting the 1937 state convention. However, there were not enough women available to work for B'nai Brith in addition to the duties they performed on behalf of other existing women's groups, so it folded.

Anti-Defamation League

In 1930, a committee consisting of Nathan Karchmer, David Schwab, and Joe Gold was appointed by the B'nai Brith to represent the Anti-Defamation League (ADL) locally. The local ADL addressed various local issues including the publication of an objectionable article in 1933 by the local paper, though they are not explicit as to what the nature of the article or its specific publication date. In response to the concern raised by the committee, the newspaper's editor, Mr. Bixly, promised such a thing would not happen again.

The ADL also appointed Mrs. H. Rubenstein and Mrs. Lester Strauss to review books in the public library for objectionable materials. The ladies discovered some objectionable material in 1935 and the matter was passed to the B'nai Brith Public Relations committee. The ADL then requested a copy of *The Rise and Destiny of the German Jew* be donated to the library, along with a copy of *The International Jew*. It subsequently expanded its book donations to both Drury College, Southwest Missouri State Teachers College (now Missouri State University), and School of the Ozarks.

Interfaith Work

Rabbi Zucker in the 1980s was well aware of the Assemblies of God Church's feelings about Jews. The Assemblies of God, whose headquarters are in Springfield, mission is to "evangelize the lost"[7] and they believe that they are tolerant because Jews can come freely to Jesus. Missionary Robert Specture is clear that "to know that following Jesus, the King of the Jews

Temple Israel congregant removing paint from headstones after the desecration of cemetery in 2001. *Courtesy Springfield News-Leader.*

and the Messiah, is the most naturally Jewish thing they [Jews] can do."[8] Zucker and Stanley Anderman from the St. Louis ADL attempted to set up a dialogue with an Assemblies of God representative. Zucker and Rabbi Leon Klenecki, Director of Interfaith Affairs for the ADL met with a representative of the Assemblies of God to discuss their film *Twice Chosen* that is part of the mission to convert Jews. It is unclear what resulted from these meetings. In the early 2000s, however, professors Lois Olena, Robert Berg, and Wave Nunnally from Evangel University—an AG-affiliated institution—built relationships with Rabbi Rita Sherwin in an effort to develop more fruitful ties between the faith communities.

In 1986, the Jewish community realized that they needed a liaison to work with the local school system. It interpreted certain activities—like religious art being encouraged around Christmas time and homecoming celebrations on the Jewish High Holy days—as antisemitic, though the offenses were likely unintentional. Cindy Rushefsky formed an ad hoc committee in 1987 "to deal with Christianity in the schools."[9] Later that year it became a standing committee. In 1988, the committee met with the superintendent of Springfield Public Schools. Best known for breaking the local school district's "good-old-boy system," Dr. Paul Hagerty responded to the committee's concerns by creating "an internal committee to deal with religious issues."[10]

In 2001, synagogue president Margo Hudson met with Jack Ernst, the school superintendent, because a feeling of exclusion among the Jewish students endured. Ernest promised to make the school calendar "sensitive" to the Jewish calendar and invited Rabbi Sherwin to do some staff training.[11] In 2003, Rabbi Sherwin met with the calendar committee of the Springfield Public Schools to ensure it was not exclusionary. For a time after this meeting, the synagogue sent a letter to the Springfield Public School calendar committee that provided the Jewish holy days to avoid further confusion. When Norm Ridder became the new school superintendent in 2005, Irwin Cohen, Marla Marantz, Susan Waxman, and Rabbi Sherwin met with him because of some remarks he had made about the role of religion in the classroom that the Jewish community found objectionable.

On February 6, 2001, vandals desecrated the Temple Israel cemetery by scrawling swastikas and other SS symbols in red spray paint on the headstones. This was not the first time. The first recorded desecration of the Temple Israel cemetery was during the summer of 1974, but nothing more is known. Again, there was a desecration reported to the board at the March 5, 1978 meeting. The incident 2001 desecration would be one of the 65 hate crimes reported in Missouri for 2001 and the only one in the city against a religious group.

The hate crime, officially called ethnic intimidation, was reported at 8 A.M. Brian Hamburg, the president of the synagogue, was "disturbed" and "stunned." A lifelong resident of Springfield, he was "generally . . . impressed that most people here are accepting of the local Jewish community, but I was keenly aware that a small part of this community harbors antisemitic sentiment."[12] The cemetery warden,

Temple Israel's first liaison to the Interfaith Alliance, Irwin Cohen. *Courtesy Telling Traditions Project.*

World War II veteran, and husband of a Holocaust refugee, Chaim Lotven, was thankful only property was damaged and not people because "that would bother me far more."[12] For him, in Judaism, greater importance is placed on the living, than the dead: "It is stone. It is brick. It is mortar."[13] By 1 P.M., representatives from various religious-based organizations, including the Council of Churches (CC) and the Ministerial Alliance, were at the cemetery to begin cleaning the headstones. Charlie Bahn, president of the Ministerial Alliance, was "shocked and horrified" and believed that by helping to scour the headstones the Christian community could prove that such actions would not be tolerated.[14] The CC paid for professional cleaning of the headstones as Dorsey Levell, the executive director at the time, felt that it was "our problem; not yours."[15] Hamburg appreciated that this was "heartfelt" and a statement "against intolerance in Springfield, Missouri. I found this offer to be very sincere, and it was quite welcome."[16] The CC continued to receive donations for a while after announcing their intention to pay for the cleaning.

The Christian community was outraged. Fr. Andrew Moore, of the American Orthodox Church in Springfield, told his son and the public in an editorial to the paper that the perpetrators "went away in the dark because they're afraid to be seen in the light."[17] Kenneth Chumbley, rector of Christ Episcopal Church, called on his fellow Christians "to befriend our Jewish [neighbors and] . . . learn to understand, respect, and indeed celebrate their history, beliefs, and traditions, which are the womb of our own."[18] The local paper published an editorial by the staff calling the locals out to eradicate the racism and antisemitism that "simmer[s] too close to the surface."[19] Another article published the day of the rededication reminded the community to attend because "it is an opportunity for us to stand as brothers and sisters. It is an opportunity for us to face the blemishes in our city, and vow to erase them."[20]

On February 11, the cemetery was rededicated by Rabbi Rita Sherwin, leader of the Springfield synagogue at the time, and many community members. President Hamburg made sure that his statement at the event "focus[ed] on the response. I recognized our appreciation for the kindness extended by the Council of Churches to be responsible for the cleanup, and the solidarity we felt with the members of the community who stood with us."[21]

Not long after, law enforcement questioned six teenagers in connection with the crime, their houses searched, and they were given lie detector tests.

In May, a representative from the Greene County Sheriff's Department attended a Board meeting to report on the "'ongoing investigation'. . . [concerning] antisemitic activity in the area."[22] The lawyer for the ADL met with the police chief to discuss the issue. However, no one was ever arrested for the crime. Some residents of the city tied the crime to a beating of an African American by two Nazi-tattooed men around the same time. Most importantly, to our discussion, is that some members of the Jewish community preferred not to discuss the incident. Lotven told the local press, "I think we should leave it alone."[23] However, there were other congregants who could not and would not "let it be." In a letter to the newspaper, Francie Wolff, whose father escaped Nazi Germany in the mid-1930s, becoming an outspoken member of the National Association for the Advancement of Colored People (NAACP), rejected the advice to "not publicly reveal" her feelings because "if we minimize our outrage, we are burying our heads in Ozarks sand" and permitting anti-Semites to regain power.[24] As Karen Aroesty, the Missouri regional director for the ADL, noted, the tolerance of hate crimes are a reflection of sorts of values a community may collectively hold.

The Interfaith Alliance was founded after the desecration of the Temple Israel cemetery as an effort "to promote a better understanding among the various religious groups within the Springfield community in order to achieve a greater respect for each other."[25] The group held a community meal almost immediately after its creation and the rabbi was impressed that "the Interfaith fellowship project is furthering a rewarding relationship between the Jewish and the Christian communities" after only two months in existence.[26] The first four member religious groups were: Christ Episcopal Church, Deliverance Temple, Brentwood Christian Church, and Temple Israel. Christ Episcopal Church, Deliverance Temple (a mostly African American church), and Temple Israel were already participating in a monthly dialogue. Their mission was to "develop mutual understanding, respect, and trust within the faith communities" through conversation and education.[27] Irwin Cohen was the first synagogue member to be the congregation's liaison with the group. Currently, not only is the Council of Churches represented on this board, but so are the Jews, Muslims, Baha'i, and various Christian denominations. However, as a recent Jewish representative Sue Conine noted, it does not have "an effect on the population as a whole" because "those who hate us [Jews] would not be part of this group."[28]

Swastika discovered on the campus of Central High School. *Courtesy Sasha Cohen Ioannides.*

Springfield religious leaders also formed a local chapter of Clergy Against Hate after the cemetery desecration. Its purpose was to "be a vehicle of rapid response as hate crimes occur in the community."[29] Clergy Against Hate was a national organization formed by religious leaders of many faiths across the United States to fight "hate-motivated violence . .. [in their] communities."[30] This group seems to have ceased to exist after the passing of the Matthew Shepard Local Law Enforcement Hate Crimes Prevention Act of 2007.

Complaints arose again in 2005 about antisemitic comments being made in the schools and parents asked the synagogue to provide education to the children on how to respond. The school board responded by bringing the ADL's Karen Aroesty to speak to the Religious School. In 2007, there was an incident in one of the public schools where a child used racial epitaphs against a Jewish child. The director of the school believed the language that was used was cruel but not intentionally antisemitic and denied that there was antisemitism in the school.

In May of 2015, a swastika was found on the Central High School campus by a Jewish student. The student was told by some faculty to not report the incident because it was not that important. The implication being that the person who painted the design really did not understand the impact of their work. The representative from the ADL agreed with the supposition of the faculty but began working with the school to create awareness about why the swastika is such a painful and hateful symbol.

Hadassah

Around 1973, Teresa Tarrasch recently arrived, and daughter-in-law to Ernest and Ena Tarrasch, approached Rabbi Smith's wife Hannah about starting a chapter of Hadassah in Springfield. She was enthusiastic and in October 1974 the chapter was founded. The first president was Bobbi Lurie who was instrumental in getting the group organized.

Hadassah, the Women's Zionist Organization of America, was founded in 1912 by Henrietta Szold. Henrietta had just returned from a visit to the Holy Land where she discovered Jews living in deplorable conditions and decided something had to be done. The mission of the organization is to offer medical care in Israel.

Teresa, a later president of the group, does not believe that the members of Hadassah were particularly Zionist, but they were very interested in learning about Israel. Most of the Hadassah members were also members of the Sisterhood, although a few were Christian. These Christian members, though welcomed, were also viewed with a hint of suspicion.

The point of the Hadassah chapters is to help fund the work Hadassah does in Israel and elsewhere. Thus, their main goal is to fundraise. In a small Jewish community, like Springfield, this was problematic. Therefore, to differentiate themselves from the Sisterhood they sponsored an annual art auction.

In 1986, with a membership of 24, Hadassah took on the task of freeing Soviet Jews from the repression they suffered in the Soviet Union. They joined a campaign of telegrams being sent to Pres. Ronald Reagan to aid a family in getting exit visas to Israel. They also delivered Meals on Wheels. Human rights issues were a major theme of the group. On December 10, 1987, Cindy Kraft (now Platz) and Mary Chanslor led fellow Hadassah members and some non-members on a march to support Human Rights from United Hebrew Congregations to Drury University. It was broadcast on the local CBS stations and 250 balloons were released. After Rabbi Zucker gave lecture at Craig Hall on the MSU campus.

The incoming Hadassah Board of 1980, including Dianna Long and Regina Lotven. *Courtesy Dianna Long.*

In December of 1987, the group brought in the Olive Branch musical group to do a fundraising event for Hadassah Hospital in Jerusalem. Hadassah also annually participated in services in the 1980s. Because every year the international Hadassah office increased the required fundraising minimum, the chapter felt they had a financial burden that could not be met. Therefore, they disbanded.

Jewish Community Fund

In 1935, the Jewish Community Fund was founded. Irving Schwab served as the president, while the treasurer was Louis Barth. In 1938, the fund distributed $950 of aid both within the city and nationally. Shortly thereafter it ceased to exist.

National Association for the Advancement of Colored People

When Arthur Rosen arrived in Springfield in 1937, after fleeing Nazi Germany, he joined the NAACP. He may have been the only white person in Springfield's chapter at the time, but he did so because he personally understood what it was like to be excluded from society. Beginning in the 1980s more Jews joined the NAACP and took part in programs they supported.

Creation of Public Kindergarten

Fannie Arbeitman arrived in Springfield in 1935. She was disappointed that there was no public kindergarten and started work on creating one in 1936. As the mother of a toddler, she understood its importance. She and Mildred Wheeler went to the school board a number of times to request support, but they were forbidden to enter the meetings because "we were women."[31] After one of the school board members had a child, the kindergarten was approved. They received a room in the basement of Rountree Elementary School which they had to furnish themselves, although the teachers were part of the city's teaching staff. Once they had collected the donations for the furnishings, they set the price for a half day kindergarten at $3 per month and for an additional $.50 per month, they would collect the child in a station wagon.

Fannie Arbeitman.
Courtesy Springfield News-Leader.

Entertainment for Soldiers

During World War II, Edgar Herman, Nathan Karchmer, Irving Schwab, and Rabbi Richter joined the United Service Organizations. The Jewish community of Springfield reached out to the Jewish soldiers being treated at O'Reilly General Hospital. When the hospital was opened, Rabbi Richter was the Jewish community's representative at the celebration. There were Sunday afternoon socials for them at the synagogue. B'nai Brith members attended these socials to help entertain the soldiers. The B'nai Brith lodge also provided games and radios to the hospital for soldiers' amusement, and donated money—directing the Ladies Auxiliary to do the same—for storage of phonograph records at the hospital.

At least once, definitely in 1943, the community hosted a Passover Seder (ceremonial meal marking the Exodus story) at the local Young Men's Christian Association. Ruth Sussman, a University of Missouri graduate and Springfield native, volunteered at this Seder and met her future husband Leo Sigal there. They married in December before he was deployed to the South Pacific.

Jewish servicemen convalescing in Springfield celebrate Passover with Temple Israel.
Courtesy The History Museum on the Square.

Visiting Soldiers' Weddings

On July 15, 1942, Private First-Class Irving Ashton, who was stationed at Fort Leonard Wood in Missouri and Miriam Keller were married in Springfield because that was the nearest synagogue. Miriam's parents were in attendance. Apparently, Rabbi Richter followed the Reform practice of the time of not breaking a glass at the end of the ceremony. The practice of breaking the glass is a medieval tradition that has many interpretations, including a belief that it would scare away evil spirits or that it served as a reminder of the sadness after the destruction of the Temple. Miriam's father was not pleased and grabbed the glass used for the blessing of the wine and had his new son-in-law use that. The wedding party made a hasty retreat from the synagogue before they found out the consequences of that action.

In the spring of 1943, Ben and Fannie Arbeitman were asked to host the wedding of Jay Kochman, a soldier at the hospital, and Gertrude, a WAC nurse at the hospital, neither of whom had much family. Jay's mother and sister arrived from Memphis and they were the only family in attendance. Gertrude arrived in her uniform, which she then had to remove and press for the ceremony. The flowers for the event were all from the family's

Ben and Fannie Arbeitman host the wedding of Jay and Gertrude Kochman in 1943.
Courtesy The History Museum on the Square.

garden. The community pitched in with a wedding feast and the house was standing room only. The Kochmans and Arbeitmans became lifelong friends. When the Kochmans' daughter got engaged, the Arbeitmans were one of the first they called to tell.

Defense Work

Beginning in 1941, congregants joined the military in preparation to join the fight in Europe. The congregation sent 46 men to serve, a large proportion of the congregation. Hershel Rubenstein became the synagogue representative on the City Defense Council.

Jewish Federation

In 1943, the Springfield Jewish Federation was founded with "the purpose of combining fund drives."[32] They had for a number of years collected close to $40,000, but in 1978 had only gathered $5000, according to Nathan Karchmer. Their work continued until 1990. They are now defunct.

Hosting Refugees

Dr. Ernest and Ena Tarrasch and Rabbi Ernest and Annette Jacob in 1954 worked together to bring Edith Kopstein, a Holocaust refugee, to stay with the Tarrasches for a few months. Their hope was to bring some joy and positive experiences to this young lady. She had survived war torn Vienna, but barely, and when the two couples first found her she was too ill to attend school. However, after numerous care packages that included clothes and money, Edith became strong enough to pursue her educational. By bringing her to Springfield to study design and dress making, the Tarrashes and Jacobs hoped to prepare her to support her family.

Edith Kopstein. *Courtesy The History Museum on the Square.*

In the late 1970s and early 1980s, the congregation sponsored some Vietnamese immigrants. By early 1981, the congregation had sponsored 13 Vietnamese families. They also sponsored a Russian Jewish family.

Volunteering in the Community

Nathan Karchmer was one of the three men who founded the local Muscular Dystrophy Organization.

Fannie Arbeitman was the first woman on the St. John's Advisory Board (now part of the Mercy Hospital system) and volunteered at the hospital for over fifty years. She also received the Council of Churches Gift of Time Volunteer.

During the late 1990s, Temple Israel provided volunteers to work at The Kitchen, Inc. and were the only religious organization to do so. The congregation also began an annual food drive on Yom Kippur with all the donated food given to the Ozarks Food Harvest.

Brotherhood/Men's Club

The Brotherhood, whose beginnings are lost in memory, had as one of their main purposes raising money to pay the rabbi to teach an Introduction

The Latke Mavens. Joel Persky, Marc Cooper, Brian Hamburg, Mark Rushefsky, and Howard Shayne in 1997. *Courtesy Temple Israel, Springfield.*

to Judaism course at Missouri State University. This course was ultimately paid by the Chautauqua Society of St. Louis until the mid-1990s when the university finally committed to pay a professor to teach the course.

The Men's Club was formed in 1982 with 21 members. According to the synagogue board, their first projects "were the regarding of the parking lot and painting of the classrooms [at the synagogue]. They served as ushers at the High Holiday services."[33]

Part of the Men's Club was the Latke (potato pancake) Mavens (expert) who made traditional latkes for the congregation's Hanukkah Dinner. This group began when the congregation moved into "the new building" in 1996.[34] According to member Joel Persky, the idea was that "since the women cooked all the time, a group of men would get together" to take on the responsibility of "mak[ing] hundreds and hundreds" of latkes.[36] There was not any particular group organizer, though the head of the synagogue's Holiday Committee would procure the necessary ingredients. Men, including Jim Arneson, Marc Cooper, Brian Hamburg, Fred Hamburg, Joel Persky, Mark Rushefsky, Howard Shayne, Norman Simon, and Joel Waxman would gather around 7 P.M. sometime the week before the dinner and fry latkes on the synagogue

Judith Winston Peavey and Sue Winston Conine. *Courtesy Joel Waxman.*

stove and in electric skillets for up to four hours. Even though they made a huge mess that they had to clean up, it was "great fun!"[37] It seems the group stopped cooking at the turn of the millennium. Somehow people lost interest in doing it.

Community Garden

The Community Garden, on the property of Temple Israel, was an interfaith effort that was approved by the synagogue board of directors in 2005 and was started in 2006. Joel Waxman, the head of the Social Action Committee at Temple Israel, first got permission from the congregational board before approaching the local interfaith organization. Waxman had been contemplating a garden since the congregation bought the property for the synagogue. They brought in a representative from the local food bank to help plan the garden. Harry Dorman, a member of the Master Gardener Society, was a significant help. The men's club built the gardening shed with the money that the Sisterhood provided. The Ozarks Food Harvest provided starter seeds and equipment. After the first year, the interfaith community dropped out of the effort and it became an exclusively Temple Israel project.

In its first three years, the garden, which is part of the American Community Garden Association, provided over three tons of food to the Ozarks Food Harvest, an organization that furnishes food to the needy of 29 counties. In 2009, the garden won the Fain Award, which "honor[s] URJ congregations that put Jewish values to work in the world."[38]

Conclusion

This community is no different than any Jewish or non-Jewish community in the country. They serve everyone in need through charitable works. Historically, because Jews were not citizens of the countries they lived in until the early 1800s, they maintained charitable societies to support their own people. These charitable practices continued in the New World, even though Jews were now citizens of the United States. However, Jews expanded their charitable work to include everyone. Now, many of the actions the community has taken has set an example for others in the larger Springfield community.

CHAPTER VI

From the Past to the Future

SPRINGFIELD, MISSOURI IS BOTH AN anomaly and a commonality. It is the Queen City of the Ozarks on the northern cusp of the south and the southern edge of the Midwest. Once the railroad hub for the region, it is now the medical hub for the region. There are three hospitals within the city limits that have clinics around the city and branches in neighboring towns. There are three major universities in the metropolitan area, Drury, Evangel, and Missouri State, and a growing community college. What was once a village is now a small cosmopolitan midwestern city.

The area's Jewish community shares characteristics with small Jewish communities throughout the southern United States. It is these small towns that were a great influence in the development of American Judaism and poorly documented historically. In 1878, 29 percent of American Jews lived in communities like Springfield's. These Jews were part of the development of the American Midwest and far west. By 1930, only 8 percent of American Jewry lived in small Jewish communities.

When historians have studied early twentieth-century small-town America, they have overlooked the Jewish communities. However, Jews in these small towns, such as Springfield, maintained ties to the larger Jewish communities. As I have tried to show in this book, a web spread slowly across the country as Jewish families opened branches of their stores. Springfield's Jewish community was not just connected to St. Louis, but also to Cincinnati, Ohio; Piqua, Ohio; Louisville, Kentucky; and beyond.

The original Jews were German immigrants who dominated the town's stores. They integrated themselves into the larger community by joining clubs and performing community service. However, they did not forget their religious heritage and established in quick succession a cemetery, a religious congregation, and a religious school. Just as did their fellow American Jews, when Russian Jewish lives were at risk, they provided

145

succor, albeit hesitantly. They supported the Russian Jewish desire to be free, as they were made anxious about the Russians' more traditional, less emancipated ways. Soon, because of the overwhelming numbers of Russian Jewish immigrants, even Springfield's existing German Jewish population was quickly outnumbered, and an Orthodox congregation was founded.

This pattern was repeated throughout the South. The Orthodox and Reform Jews stayed separate, sometimes, as in Springfield, sharing a cemetery. The Russian Jews typically found employment as store clerks and factory workers. During the Depression, as times got rough, those who could fled the small towns, moving to the cities where economic opportunities might be more plentiful. Springfield saw an exodus of both Christians and Jews at this time. The children of Jewish immigrants were often better educated than their parents, as they were granted the advantage of an American educational system that was free to all and universities with minimal quotas. With broader horizons, few desired to remain in the Ozarks. Thus, the Jewish community in Springfield shrank.

Again, as would happen in scores of other small Jewish communities, the shrinking numbers resulted in the merging of the two congregations. Like other communities, the rigidity and old-worldliness of the Orthodox practices resulted in the Orthodox congregation folding into the Reform one, while the rising religiosity of Americans in general resulted in a more traditional Reform practice.

Unlike Southern communities, Springfield did not suffer from overt antisemitism. Jews were not excluded from the country club, or any clubs for that matter. The Ku Klux Klan in the Ozarks were mostly focused on the African Americans, of which there were few, and moral issues.

However, as is the case with other small Southern communities, the culture has been profoundly shaped by evangelical Christianity. When Springfield became the headquarters of the Assemblies of God, the tremendous influence of this mode of religious expression was not confirmed. As a result, the Springfield Jewish community has confronted more subtle forms of antisemitism, as the missionizing impulse has given rise to situations that local Jews have found disturbing if not insulting. In their zeal to convert the non-believer, evangelicals have frequently used rhetoric they might have viewed as innocuous statements that were, in fact, horribly insensitive—like "you know you are going to hell"—failing to recognize the traumas, born out of such sentiments, that have been inflicted on Jews down through the centuries.

Nevertheless, because of the hospitals, universities, and relatively low-cost of living, the Jewish community has remained viable. Many smaller Jewish communities, because they were in small towns, slowly shrank until they finally disappeared. However, because the city of Springfield continues to grow, this has not happened. Though the Jewish community peaked at about 150 households in the 1990s, it has maintained a steady size of between 100 and 120 households since the 1920s. Unlike in larger cities where families are members of the congregation for generations, Springfield has very few people who can claim membership in the congregation for multiple generations. This is due, in part, to the very factors that keep the congregation afloat—the influx of employees for the hospitals and universities. These families arrive in the region to work and retire elsewhere—usually near their extended families.

There is also the factor of intermarriage. Especially in small Jewish communities, the number of potential Jewish partners is small. Thus, many Jews marry non-Jewish locals. Thus, they may stay in the area, in this case metro-Springfield, but raised their children as Christians. Until this century, there was no other choice for couples who intermarried. In 1983, the Central Conference of American Rabbi's Committee on Patrilineal Descent revised its position, issuing the following: "The Central Conference of American Rabbis declares that the child of one Jewish parent is under the presumption of Jewish descent."[1] In doing so, the Reform Movement's leadership has hoped to encourage interfaith couples to raise their children as Jews.

With the influx of families from the coasts, the cosmopolitan nature of the Springfield community has grown. Racism and antisemitism may be tolerated in the small surrounding communities, but less so in the city. Interfaith communities work to encourage acceptance of difference—a challenge in what has historically been a notoriously xenophobic region. The number of non-Christian religions has grown in the last few decades. Springfield not only has a synagogue, but also a mosque and durga. The city boasts an American Orthodox church, as well. There are religious services held in Korean, Mandarin, and Spanish. No longer is Springfield listed as one of the ten whitest cities in the United States. All of this bodes positively for the future of the city.

There have been setbacks with small outbreaks of antisemitic graffiti, which both local leaders and Anti-Defamation League representatives believe come more from ignorance than real hatred. There are concerns that the current generation are so disconnected from history that they do not understand the fear provoked by the swastika. This, however, can be amended.

Despite the lack of social opportunities for Jewish students, the only public institute of higher learning in the city hosts a Hillel (the Hillel of Southwest Missouri). Their first actions were to work with the university to help them understand how a number of their practices, like hosting recruitment events on Jewish High Holy Days, were dissuading Jewish students from attending the university.

So long as the universities, hospitals, and relatively low cost of living continue, the synagogue will continue. It most likely will not grow, because Springfield is not a serious destination for Jews, but it will continue. Its history follows the path of many small southern Jewish communities, but its ability to remain alive sets it apart.

By putting the Jewish community into the larger context of local and American history, we gain a better understanding of how the two histories intertwine. Reconstruction was a catalyst in Jewish expansion into the West. The development of the railroad network across America provided ample opportunities for the arriving Jewish immigrants to find employment and create and influence communities. While we need to understand the history of Jews in Springfield to fully appreciate the development of American Jewry, situating this minority within the context of the broader United States history only enriches our understanding of the past. The inclusion of minority cultures in the grander narrative, again, lays bare the fiction that the colonization of the American Midwest was epitomized by figure of the white Anglo-Saxon Protestant.

NOTES

Acknowledgments

1. Board Meeting, United Hebrew Congregations, Springfield, Missouri. Minutes. February 27, 1985. OJA.

Chapter I. American Jewish History and Missouri History

1. Peter Stuyvesant to the Amsterdam Chamber of Directors, September 22, 1654, quoted in Samuel Oppenheim, *The Early History of the Jews in New York, 1654-1664: Some New Matter on the Subject* (New York: American Jewish Historical Society, 1909), 5.

2. Abraham de Lucena, Jacob Cohen Henricque, Salvador Dandrada, Joseph Dacosta, and David Frera to Director General and Council of New Amsterdam, March 14, 1656, in *New Netherland Council Minutes, 1655-1656*, vol. 6, trans. and ed. Charles T. Gehring (Syracuse, NY: Syracuse University Press, 1995), 261-262.

3. Director General and Council of New Amsterdam to Abraham de Lucena, Jacob Cohen Henricque, Salvador Dandrada, Joseph Dacosta, David Frera to, March 14, 1656, *ibid.*, 262.

4. Amsterdam Chamber of Directors to Peter Stuyvesant, March 13, 1656, in Oppenheim, *Early History of the Jews in New York*, 21.

5. Abraham de Lucena, Jacob Cohen Henricque, Salvador Dandrada, and Joseph Dacosta to Director General and Council of New Amsterdam, April 20, 1657, *ibid.*, 36.

6. An Act for Naturalizing such foreign Protestants, and others therein mentioned, as are settled or shall settle in any of his Majesty's Colonies in America., 1740, in *A Documentary History of the Jews in the United States 1654-1875*, ed. Morris U. Schappes (New York: Schocken Books, 1971), 26-30.

7. John Locke, Fundamental Constitutions of Carolina, 1669, in *ibid.*.

8. *Ibid.*

9. George Washington to the Hebrew-Congregation of the City of Savanah, 1789, in *ibid.*, 78.

10. George Washington to the Hebrew Congregation in New Port, Rhode Island, 1790, in *ibid.*, 80.

11. *Ibid.*

12. Donald I. Makovsky, *The Philipsons: The First Jewish Settlers in St. Louis 1807-1858* (St. Louis, MO: Judaism Sesquicentennial Committee of St. Louis, 1958), 8.

13. Henry R. Schoolcraft, *Journal of a Tour into the Interior of Missouri and Arkansaw,* (London: Sir Richard Phillips and Co., 1821), 54.

14. "The History of Springfield (No 6)," *Leader* [Springfield, MO], March 6, 1929, p. 14.

15. George S. Escott, *History and Directory of Springfield and North Springfield* (Springfield, MO: Patriot Advertiser, 1878), 49.

16. Brooks Blevins, *Hill Folks: A History of Arknasas Ozarkers & Their Image* (Chapel Hill: University of North Carolina Press, 2002), 18-19.

17. William J. Rountree, *Autobiography – 1932*, p. 3. Missouri Digital Heritage, n.d., cdm.sos.mo.gov/cdm/ref/collection/mack/id/3571.

18. Lyle Owen. "An Ozarker and the Jews." *Common Ground* 5 (no. 2, 1945): 3.

19. Hiram W. Evans, "The Attitude of the Knights of the Ku Klux Toward the Jew," in *Papers Read at the Meeting of Grand Dragons Knights of the Ku Klux Klan At their First Annual Meeting held at Asheville, North Carolina, July 1923*, (n.p.: E. F. Randolph, 1923 121.

20. Brooks Blevins, "The Arkansas Ghost Trial: The Connie Franklin Case and the Ozarks in the National Media," *Arkansas Historical Quarterly* 68 (Summer 2009): 251.

21. Brooks Blevins, "The Strike and the Still: Anti-Radical Violence and the Ku Klux Klan in the Ozarks," *Arkansas Historical Quarterly* 52 (Winter 1993): 406

22. Charles C. Alexander, *The Ku Klux Klan in the Southwest* (Norman: University of Oklahoma Press, 1995), 26.

23. *Constitution and Laws of the Knights of the Ku Klux Klan* (Atlanta, GA: Knights of the Ku Klux Klan, 1921), 10; A Klansman's Creed, pamphlet, n.d., p. 2, archive.lib.msu.edu/DMC/AmRad/citizensmichigan.pdf (accessed January 2, 2021).

24. Principles and Purposes of the Knights of the Ku Klux Klan, pamphlet, n.d., p. 4, archive.lib. msu.edu/DMC/AmRad/principlespurposesknights.pdf (accessed January 2, 2020).

25. Simone Lotven Sofian, "RE:anti Semitism in Springfield," email message to author, October 31, 2013.

26. Laura Scott, "Rabbi Rita Sherwin: Offering education and understanding to the community," *Today's Woman*, January 2002, p. 34.

Chapter II. Jewish Founders

1. Hasia Diner, "Entering the Mainstream of Modern Jewish History: Peddlers and the American Jewish South." *Southern Jewish History* 8 (2005): 12-13.

2. Michael A. Meyer, "German-Jewish Identity in Nineteenth-Century America," in *The American Jewish Experience*, ed. Jonathan D. Sarna (New York: Holmes & Meier, 1986), 48.

3. "Early Days in Springfield." *Republican* [Springfield, MO], May 23, 1926, n.p,

4. "Article I, Section IX, Constitution of the State of Missouri, 1865," *The Statutes of the State of Missouri*, vol. 1 (St. Louis, MO: W. J. Gilbert, 1872), 35.

5. "Article IX, Section I, Constitution of the State of Missouri, 1865," *ibid.*, 58.

6. "L. Ullman," advertisement. *Missouri Weekly Patriot* [Springfield, MO] January 31, 1867, p. 1.

7. "An Act to Encourage Immigration to the State of Missouri," *First Report to the Board of Immigration of the State of Missouri to the Twenty-four General Assembly* (Jefferson City, MO: Emory S. Foster, 1867), 3.

8. *Opening of the Atlantic and Pacific Railroad and completion of South Pacific Railroad to Springfield, MO, May 3, 1870* (Springfield, MO: n.p., 1870), 7 [first quotation], 8 [second quotation].

9. "The Railroad. First Train Over the Ozark Mountains," *Springfield Leader* [MO] April 28, 1870, p. 3

10. "Victor Sommers," *Missouri Weekly Patriot* [Springfield, MO] December 30, 1875, p. 2.

11. Return Ira Holcombe, *History of Greene County, Missouri* (St. Louis, MO: Western Historical Company, 1883), 545.

12. George S. Escott, *History and Directory of Springfield and North Springfield* (Springfield, MO: Patriot Advertiser, 1878), 112.

13. *Ibid.*

14. *The History of Miami County, Ohio* (Chicago: W. H. Beers Co., 1880), 452.

15. "Married, at Carthage yesterday..." *Springfield Leader* [MO] May 1886: n.pag

16. "Mrs. Emmanuel Mars." *Herald* [Springfield, MO] 27 Sept. 1887. In *Abstracts of Items of Genealogical Interest from the Springfield, Greene County, MO newspapers for 1887 and 1884*. Edited by William K. Hall (St. Louis: n.p., 1993), 102.

17. "Moses Levy." *History of Saline County Missouri* (St. Louis: Missouri Historical Co., 1881), 759-560.

18. "Daniel H. Herman." *Republican* [Springfield, MO], February 1, 1908, p. 5.

19. "Pioneer is Dead." *Springfield Missouri Republican* 15 Sep. 1926, p. 1.

20. "Son born to E." *Leader* [Springfield, MO] December 30, 1889, in *Abstracts of Items of Genealogical Interest from the Springfield, Greene County, MO Newspapers for 1889*, ed. William K. Hall (St. Louis, MO: n.p., 1994), 235.

21. *Pictorial and Genealogical Record of Greene County, Missouri* (Chicago: Goodspeed Brothers, 1893), 390.

22. *Ibid.*

23. *Ibid.*, 28-29 [quotations, 29].

24. "The swellest society event," *Leader-Democrat* [Springfield, MO] September 23, 1897, p. 8; "The marriage of Miss Della Levy," *Springfield Missouri Republican*, September 23, 1897, p. 5.

25. "Jacob Rothschild Dies at Home Here After Long Illness." *Leader* [Springfield, MO] May 15, 1925, p. 1.

26. "Moses Levy Dies at Age of 81." *Leader* [Springfield, MO] February 20, 1928, p. 1.

Chapter III. The Second Community

1. He chose this spelling of his name after a fight with his father.

2. "St. Louis and the Southwest," *American Hatter*, August 1909, p. 112.

3. Mike Sussman, draft registration, Springfield, MO, 1917 familysearch.org/ ark:/61903/1:1:K3T3-2XR (accessed September 29, 2015).

4. Fannie Arbeitman, interview by Julie Hennigan, January 9, 1993, transcript. OJA. Ozarks Jewish Archives, Special Collections and Archives, Missouri State University, Springfield, MO [hereinafter OJA].

5. Lefkowitz, David. "The Duty of the Home." *American Israelite*, April 12, 1917.

6. "Expansion is Planned," *Springfield Missouri Republican*, April 14, 1926, p. 1.

7. "Gordon-Samors," *Republican* [Springfield, MO], June 3, 1923, p. 3.

Chapter IV. Creation of a Religious Community

1. "'The American Jews' Synopsis of a Lecture by Rabbi H. Berkowitz, D.D., of Kansas City," *Springfield Daily Democrat* [MO], March 15, 1892, p. 4.

2. *Temple Israel Board Minutes* (Springfield, MO: Temple Israel, 1914-1960), 40,

3. Nathan Karchmer, interviewed by Julie Hennigan, January 18, 1993, interview 2, transcript. OJA.

4. Clara Ullman, letter to the editor, *The Sabbath Visitor*, July 23, 1875, p. 116.

5. Isaac Wise, "The Confirmation and the Bar Mitzvah," *Asmonean* 1854, in *The Jews in the Modern World: A Documentary History*, 3rd ed., eds. Paul Mendes-Flohr and Jehuda Reinharz (New York: Oxford University Press, 2010), 518-519.

6. *Temple Israel Board Minutes.* 13-14 [quotation, p. 13], OJA.

7. Cemetery Rules (Springfield, MO: United Hebrew Congregations, 1985), 1, OJA.

8. "Rosh Hassanah," *Springfield Democrat* September 12, 1893, p. 1.

9. "Jewish Services," *Springfield Weekly Republication*, October 11, 1894, p. 4.

10. *Temple Israel Board Minutes,* 58, OJA.

11. *Ibid.*, 70, OJA.

12. Ernest Israel Jacob, "Fifty Years of Jewish Life in Springfield, MO," in *Fifty Years: Temple Israel, Springfield, Missouri* (Springfield, MO: Temple Israel, 19 November 1943), 2.

13. Irving Schwab to Members of United Hebrew Congregations, February 17, 1950, letter, OJA.

14. Temple Israel Kitchen & Food, pamphlet, November 14, 1995, *ibid.*

15. Fannie Arbeitman, Interview by Julie Hennigan. Springfield MO, January 9, 1993, Transcript. OJA.

16. B'nai Brith Lodge 717, June 2, 1948, minutes, OJA.

17. Hyman Lotven and Isadore Lotven. Interview by Julie Hennigan. Springfield, MO. 21 December 1992. Transcript. OJA.

18. Stuart Federow, telephone interview with author, October 6, 2013.

19. Stuart Federow, *Judaism and Christianity: A Contrast* (Bloomington, IN: iUniverse, 2012), xiii.

20. Board meeting, Temple Israel, August 20, 2005, minutes, OJA.

21. Board of directors meeting, United Hebrew Congregations, September 7, 1986, minutes, OJA.

22. Building committee, United Hebrew Congregations, February 19, 1989, report, p. 2, OJA.

23. Joel Persky to Friends, October 19, 1995, letter, OJA..

24. Committee to Evaluate the Constitution and By-laws. July 1976, letter, OJA.

25. Board meeting, United Hebrew Congregations, June 29, 1970, minutes, p. 2, OJA.

26. Board meeting, United Hebrew Congregations, November 22, 1972, minutes, p. 1, OJA.

27. Committee to Evaluate the Constitution and By-laws, 2. OJA.

28. Temple Israel Board Minutes, p. 55. OJA.

29. Board meeting, United Hebrew Congregations, December 26, 1973, minutes, p. 1, OJA.

30. Irving Schwab to Harry S. Truman, December 30, 1938, letter, Harry S. Truman Presidential Library, Independence, MO.

31. *Ibid.* [first and third quotations]

32. Christopher Goffard, "Keeper of Faith." *Tampa Bay Times*, [FL] April 21, 2005, www.sptimes. com/2005/04/21/Floridian/Keeper_of_faith.shtml (accessed December 3, 2013).

33. David Richter, email message to author, January 9, 2010.

34. Lester Strauss, Report of the President of Temple Israel, September 28, 1941, p. 2, OJA.

35. Chapter 227 State Highway System. Sec. 227.410, August 28, 2013, *Missouri Revised Statutes.*

36. Yearly membership meeting, Temple Israel, February 8, 1970, minutes, p. 2, OJA.

37. Ruth Rubenstein, interview by Julie Hennigan. February 24, 1993, transcript, OJA.

38. Gerrit J. tenZythoff, to Jerome Caplan, January 21, 1975, letter, OJA.

39. Rubenstein interview.

40. Council of Churches of the Ozarks, "Company Overview," Facebook, www.facebook.com/ccozarks/ (accessed July 27, 2015).

41. Council of Churches of the Ozarks, "Mission," Facebook, www.facebook.com/ccozarks/ (accessed July 27, 2015).

42. Neil Stenger to Stefan Broidy, December 11, 1987, letter, Jacob Rader Marcus Center of the American Jewish Archives, Hebrew Union College, Cincinnati, OH.

43. Kathleen O'Dell, "Springfield congregation to install first female rabbi." *News-Leader* [Springfield, MO], July 30, 1992.

44. Hope V. Stewart, "The Lady Is a Rabbi!" *Springfield!* (1992): 35.

45. Congregational meeting, Temple Israel, April 20, 2003, minutes, OJA.

46. Central Conference of American Rabbis. Resolution on Same Gender Officiation. CCAR, March 2000, www.ccarnet.org/rabbis-speak/resolutions/2000/same-gender-officiation/ (accessed June 6, 2015).

47. Dorsey E. Level, "Thank You," April 1, 1995, certificate.

Chapter V. Charity and Community Service

1. *Programme of the Springfield Ladies Saturday Club for 1891-1892* (Springfield, MO: Charles Nevatt, 1891), 16, Ladies Saturday Club Collection? The History Museum on the Square, Springfield, MO.

2. Ladies Aid Society, business meetings book, 1924-1933, p. 20. OJA.

3. *Ibid.*, 98.

4. Albert C. Stevens, ed. *The Cyclopedia of Fraternities* (New York: Hamilton Printing, 1899), 142.

5. "Death Claims Business Man of Springfield," *Leader*, [Springfield MO] January 23, 1930, evening edition, p. 16.

6. B'nai Brith minutes book. Springfield, MO, 1926-1962, p. 55, OJA.

7. "About Us." *Assemblies of God USA*. 1995-2013. Accessed October 15, 2013, http://ag.org/top/mobile/About.

8. "Summer outreach--the Jewish community." *Assemblies of God News*. June 7, 2001. Accessed October 2013, http://ag.org/top/News/index_articledetail.cfm?Process=DisplayArticle&targetBay =c97d4d5c-a325-4921-9a9e-

9. "Who are The Assemblies of God, and what do they have to do with the Jews?" *Jews for Judaism*, n.d., jewsforjudaism.org/knowledge/articles/who-are-the-assemblies-of-god-and-what-do-they-have-to-do-with-the-jews/ (accessed January 5, 2021).

10. Martha Miller, "Educator Made Schools Tougher and Watched Test Scores Leap." *Orlando*

Sentinel, April 30, 1992. articles.orlandosentinel.com/1992-04-30/news/9204300429_1_hagerty-elementary-schools-springfield (accessed May 25, 2015); Board meeting, United Hebrew Congregations, October 30, 1988, minutes, p. 2, OJA.

11. Board meeting, Temple Israel, August 19, 2001, minutes, OJA; Board meeting, Temple Israel, February 16, 2003, minutes, p. 1, OJA.

12. Brian Hamburg, "Re: president during the cemetery desecration." Email to author. October 20, 2013.

13. Angela Wilson, "Ceremony today at vandalized cemetery." *Springfield News-Leader* [Missouri] February 11, 2001: A10.

14. Linda Leicht, "Religious groups work together." *Springfield News-Leader* [Missouri] February 7, 2001: A9.

15. Hamburg, "Re: president during"

16. *Ibid.*

17. "In the face of hatred: love." *Springfield News-Leader* [Missouri] February 7, 2001, Our View sec.

18. *Ibid.*

19. *Ibid.*

20. "Community's true cleanup begins today." *Springfield News-Leader* [Missouri] February 11, 2001.

21. Hamburg, *Ibid.*

22. Board Meeting. Temple Israel, Springfield, Missouri. Minutes. May 13, 2001. OJA.

23. Linda Leicht, "Graves defiled: a man thrice stabbed." *Springfield News-Leader* [MO] April 28, 2002: A4.

24. Francie Wolff, "Don't dismiss an act of hatred." *Springfield News-Leader* [MO] February 9, 2001, Opinion sec.

25. 2001 Interfaith Annual Report, Temple Israel, congregational meeting, April 7, 2001, OJA; for more on the Interfaith Alliance, see Chapter 3: "Creation of a Jewish Community."

26. Congregational meeting, Temple Israel, April 7, 2001, OJA.

27. Interfaith Alliance of the Ozarks, n.d, sites.google.com/site/ozarksfaith/ (accessed October 24, 2013).

28. Sue Conine, "Re: Interfaith alliance," email message to author, October 15, 2013.

29. Board meeting, Temple Israel, minutes, August 19, 2001, OJA.

30. Clergy Against Hate, "LLEHCPA Sign-On Letter to Senator," July 11, 2007, civilrights.org, www.civilrights.org/hatecrimes/llehcpa/2007/clergy.html (accessed November 25, 2013).

31. Jennifer Ready, "Fannie Arbeitman and the Springfield Demonstration Kindergartens." *OzarksWatch 12.* (no. 1/2, 1999): 18-20.

32. Board meeting, United Hebrew Congregations, March 5, 1978, minutes, OJA.

33. Board meeting. United Hebrew Congregations, February 13, 1983, minutes, p. 2, *ibid.*

34. Marc Cooper, interview, February 18, 2003, recording, OJA.

36. Joel Persky, interview, February 13, 2003, recording, OJA.

37. *Ibid.*

38. "Fain Awards: FAQs," Religious Action Center of Reform Judaism, www.rac.org/fainawards-faqs (accessed May 15, 2015).

Chapter VI. From the Past to the Future

1. Committee on Patrilineal Descent, "Reform Movement's Resolution on Patrilineal Descent," March 15, 1983. www.jewishvirtuallibrary.org/jsource/Judaism/patrilineal1.html (accessed May 13, 2011).

REFERENCES

Abbreviations

OJA—Ozarks Jewish Archives, Special Collections and Archives, Missouri State University, Springfield, MO.

THMOTS—The History Museum on the Square, Springfield, MO.

Autobiography/Biography

Arbeitman, Fannie. Interview by Julie Hennigan. January 9, 1993. OJA.

Biographies of Pioneer Members of Anshe Emeth Jewish Temple, Piqua, 1962. Piqua, OH: Anshe Emeth Congregation, 1962. Jacob Rader Marcus Center of American Jewish Archives, Cincinnati, OH.

Chowning, Robert W. "Biography of Max Yoffie." *History of St. Francis County, Arkansas.* Forest City, Arkansas: Weston McCollum Lewey, 1954.

Cooper, Marc. Recorded interview. February 18, 2003. OJA.

"David M. Oberman." *Biographies from Cole County People.* Cole County Historical Society, 2006-2015. Accessed April 21, 2015. www.colecohistsoc.org/bios/bio_o.html.

Fetter, Bernard. Interview by Julie Hennigan. February 19, 1993. Transcript. OJA.

Jacob, Walter. Personal interview. September 20, 2007.

_____. "Rabbi in Two Worlds." in *Paths of Faithfulness: A Collection of Sermons by Ernest I. Jacob,* xvi-xxviii. Edited by Walter Jacob and Herbert Jacob. Pittsburgh: n.p., 1964.

Karchmer, Nathan. Interview 1 by Julie Henigan. January 5, 1993. Transcript. OJA.

_____. Interview 2 by Julie Henigan. January 18, 1993. Transcript. OJA.

Levy, Bennie. 1894. Headstone. Sedalia Hebrew Union Cemetery.

Levy, Millie. 1891. Headstone. Sedalia Hebrew Union Cemetery.

Lotven, Isadore. Interview by Julie Hennigan. March 3, 1993. Transcript. OJA.

Lotven, Israel, Mike Sussman, and Julius Bookman. 1912. Photograph. Courtesy of Regina Lotven.

Lotven, Hyman. *My Life Story*. Springfield, MO: The Ethnic Life Stories Project, 2001.

Lotven, Hyman and Isadore Lotven. Interview by Julie Hennigan. December 21, 1992. Transcript. OJA.

Lurie, Hal. Interview by Julie Hennigan. March 2, 1993. Transcript. OJA.

"Moses Levy." *History of Saline County Missouri*. St. Louis: Missouri Historical Co., 1881.

Nathan, Infant. February 1901. Headstone. Temple Israel Cemetery, Springfield, MO.

Raskin, Lorraine Lipman. Telephone interview. February 15, 2012.

Ready, Jennifer. "Fannie Arbeitman and the Springfield Demonstration Kindergartens." *OzarksWatch* 12.1&2 (1999): 18-20.

Rosenbaum, Walter. Interview, March 9, 2012.

Rountree, William J. "Autobiography –1932," p. 2. Missouri Digital Heritage, n.d., cdm.sos.mo.gov/cdm/ref/collection/mack/id/3571.

Rubenstein, Ruth. Interview by Julie Hennigan. February 24, 1993. Transcript. OJA.

Rushefsky, Mark. Recorded interview. 5 March 2003. OJA.

Sass, Sarah. Interview by Julie Hennigan. January 18, 1993. Transcript. OJA.

Schwab Bros. Clothing. Photograph. ©1908. Archives Photo Col., Business, box 7, folder 13. THMOTS.

Schwab, Stephen. Telephone interview. April 11, 2012.

Rosenwasser, Rabbi Herman. Headstone. Congregation Agudus Achim Cemetery, San Antonio, TX.

"Ruth Sigal." Obituary. U-T San Diego February 24, 2013. Accessed 21 April 2015, www.obitsforlife.com/obituary/639729/Sigal-Ruth.php.

Schoolcraft, Henry Rowe. *Journal of a Tour into the Interior of Missouri and Arkansaw*, London: Richard Phillips & Co., 1921.

Scharff, Rosa. October 15, 1889. Headstone. Natchez City Cemetery, Natchez, MS.

Ullman, Lee. September 13, 1929. Headstone. Saint Mary's Cemetery, Springfield, MO.

Ullman, Sara Maas. April 19, 1896. Headstone. Hazelwood Cemetery, Springfield, MO.

United Hebrew Congregations. 1944-1994. Plaque. Temple Israel, Rogersville, MO.

Correspondence

Ashton, Dianne. Re: Hannukkah [*sic*] story. Email message to author. February 6, 2008.

Bisman, Ida. Letter to Harold H. Lurie. October 13, 1973. OJA.

Bisman, Robert I. and Harold H. Lurie. Letter to the Membership of the United Hebrew Congregations. May 12, 1972. OJA.

Burstin, Kenneth. Email message to author. July 6, 2015.

____. Email message to author. August 22, 2012.

Committee to Evaluate the Constitution and By-laws. Letter to Member. July 1976. OJA.

Cooper, Marc. Letter to Rabbi c.1984. OJA.

Crow, John C. Letter to Jim Winnerman. March 9, 1981. OJA.

Freiberg, Burton. Letter to Mrs. Minnie Hirsch. September 25, 1933. OJA.

____. Letter to Mr. & Mrs. J. L. Rubenstein. April 20. 1931. OJA.

Goldin, Paula. Letter to Linda Joyce Leavitt. January 19. 1983. OJA.

Hirsch, Minnie. Letter to Cousin Sadie. *The Sabbath Visitor* May 1886: 639.

Jonas, Joseph. Letter to Isaac Lesser. December 25, 1843. Reprint "The Jews in Ohio, by Joseph Jonas, an autobiographical account, December 25, 1843." *A Documentary History of the Jews in the United States 1654-1875.* Edited by Morris U. Schappes. New York: Schocken Books, 1971. 224.

Kaplan, Regina H. Letter to Burton Freiberg. September 30, 1949. OJA.

Karchmer, Lorena. Letter to President and Trustees of Temple Israel. September 25, 1941. OJA.

Karchmer, William. Letter to Robert C. Kramer. June 4, 1976. OJA.

Klass, Julia Cohn. Letter to niece or nephew. n.d. Private collection.

Kramer, Robert C. Letter to Hyman Lotven. June 4, 1976. OJA.

Major, Elliott W. Letter to Senate of the 48th General Assembly of the State of Missouri. February 10, 1915. Reprinted in *Journal of the Senate of the Forty-Eighth General Assembly of the State of Missouri.* Jefferson City: State of Missouri, 1915. 342.

"Passover Seder at YMCA." Springfield, Missouri. Spring 1943. Photograph. THMOTS.

Persky, Joel. Recorded interview. February 13, 2003. OJA.

Persky, Joel. Letter to Friends. October 19, 1995. OJA.

Richter, David. Email message to author. January 9, 2010.

Robbins, Liz. "Re: Contact Request—Garland County Historical Society." Email message to author. January 31. 2011.

Rope, Harry L., Sam Fayman, and Burton Freiberg. Letter to J. L. Rubenstein. October 29, 1943. OJA.

Rosen, Mark. Letter to Rabbi David Wucher. February 19, 1980. OJA.

Schwab, Irving. Letter to Members of United Hebrew Congregations.

February 17, 1950. OJA.

____. Letter to Harry S. Truman. December 30, 1938. Harry S. Truman Library. Independence, MO.

Simon, James L. Letter to Ruth Grant. January 8, 1988. OJA.

Sofian, Simone Lotven. Email message to author. October 31, 2013.

Soskin, Dianne. Telephone interview. April 19, 2012.

tenZythoff, Gerrit J. Letter to Jerome Caplan. January 21, 1975. OJA.

Tarrasch, Teresa. Telephone interview. July 11, 2015.

Truman, Harry S. Letter to Samuel W. Honaker. January 5, 1939. Harry S. Truman Library. Independence, MO.

Ullman, Clara. Letter. *The Sabbath Visitor* [Cincinnati], July 23, 1875: 116.

Watters, Jim and Mary Moskowitz Watters. Telephone interview. April 4, 2012.

Waxman, Joel. Re: "Garden History." Email message to author. May 17, 2015.

Weiss, Marlita. Telephone interview. August 5, 2012.

____. E-mail to author, August 2, 2011.

White, Andrew. Dispatch to Walter Q. Gresham. July 6, 1893. Reprint in *The American Jew as Patriot, Soldier and Citizen*. Edited by Simon Wolf. Cranbury, NJ: Scholar's Bookshelf, 2006. 528.

Wucher, David. Letter to the author. June 27, 2011.

Zucker, David J. E-mail to author. May 22, 2015.

Demographic Materials

Altschul, Isaac. Campbell Township, Springfield City, Ward 1, 4, Greene, Missouri, United States Census, 1900, sheet 22A.

Altschul, Solomon. Ohio, United States Census, 1870, p. 40.

Arbetman, Nathan. Springfield, Greene, Missouri, United States Census, 1930, sheet 1B.

Arbitman, William. Springfield, Greene, Missouri, United States Census, 1930, sheet 6A.

Barker and Escott. *Springfield and North Springfield City Directory for 1884-5*. Springfield, Missouri: Stephens & Means, 1884.

Bernheimer, Charles S. "Summary of Jewish Organizations in the United States." *American Jewish Year Book*, Vol. 2. Philadelphia: Jewish Publication Society, 1900. 496-506.

Bookman, Judas. Area G, Tulsa, Tulsa City, Tulsa, Oklahoma, United States Census, 1940, sheet 2B.

Bookman, Julius. Picher, Ottowa, Oklahoma, United States Census, 1930, sheet 8B.

Breadman, Bertha. Ward 4, Springfield, Campbell Township, Greene, Missouri, United States Census, 1940, sheet 62B.

Bredman, Ida. Springfield, Greene, Missouri, United States Census, 1930, sheet 2B.

Chenkin, Alvin. "Jewish Population in the United States, 1959." *American Jewish Year Book*. Vol. 61. Philadelphia: Jewish Publication Society, 1960. 3-10.

City Directory 1909. Springfield, Missouri: Inland Printing, 1909.

Cohen, Morris. Marshfield, Webster County, Missouri, United States Census, 1880, sheet 356B.

Cohn, Isaac. Springfield Ward 2, Greene, Missouri, United States Census, 1920, sheet 7A.

Cohn, Julius. Missouri. United States Census, 1870, p. 35.

"Directories & Lists." *American Jewish Year Book*, Vol. 38. Philadelphia: Jewish Publication Society, 1936. 449-551.

Driben, Samuel, St. Louis, St. Louis, Missouri, United States Census, 1880, sheet 308B.

Dunham's Springfield, MO City Directory 1914. Springfield: Dunham Directory Co., 1914.

Dunham's Springfield, MO City Directory 1915. Springfield, Missouri: Dunham Directory Co., 1915.

Dunham's Springfield, MO City Directory 1916. Springfield: Dunham Directory Co., 1916.

Dunham's Springfield, MO City Directory 1917. Springfield: Dunham Directory Co., 1917.

1881 Directory of Springfield. St. Louis: US Directory Publishing, 1881.

1873 Springfield City Directory. St. Louis: R. P. Studley Co., 1873.
Ellman, Ben
St. Louis City, Missouri, United States Census, 1910, sheet 2B.

Ellman, Benj. Springfield Ward 2, Greene, Missouri, United States Census, 1920, sheet 14A.

Ellman, Benjamin. St. Louis (Independence City), Missouri, United States Census, 1930, sheet 23B.

Escott, George S. *History and Directory of Springfield and North Springfield*. Springfield, Missouri Patriot Advertiser, 1878.

Glaser, Ignace. Campbell Township, Springfield City, Ward 2, Greene, Missouri, United States census, 1900, sheet 21B.

____. Springfield, Ward 4, Greene, Missouri, United States census 1910, sheet 9A.

Glaser, Ignas. Springfield, Greene, Missouri, United States Census, 1930, sheet 16B.

Goldstein, Sidney. "Population Trends in American Jewry." *Judaism* 36.2 (1987): 135.

Herman, Daniel H. Missouri, United States Census, 1900, sheet 22A.

Herman, Henry. New York, United States Census, 1870, page 95.

Hirsch, Simon. Campbell Township, Springfield City Ward 2, Greene, Missouri, United States Census 1900, sheet 26A.

_____. St. Louis Ward 23, St. Louis (Independent City), Missouri, United States Census, 1910, sheet 5A.

Hirschland, Benj. Des Moines Township, Precinct 4 Des Moines city Ward 3, Polk, Iowa, United States Census, 1900, sheet 2B.

Hirschland, Charles. Campbell Township, Springfield city Ward 1, 4, Greene, Missouri, United States Census, 1900, sheet 30A.

Hoffman, Samuel. Toledo, Ohio, United States Census, 1870, page 34.

Hoye's City Directory of Springfield, MO. Kansas City, MO: Hoye Directory Co., 1888.

Hoye's City Directory of Springfield, MO. Kansas City, MO: Hoye Directory Co., 1890.

Hoye's City Directory of Springfield, MO. Kansas City, MO: Hoye Directory Co., 1892.

Hoye's City Directory of Springfield, MO. Kansas City, MO: Hoye Directory Co., 1894.

Hoye's City Directory of Springfield, MO. Kansas City, MO: Hoye Directory Co., 1895.

Hoye's City Directory of Springfield, MO. Kansas City, MO: Hoye Directory Co., 1898.

Hoye's City Directory of Springfield, MO. Kansas City, MO: Hoye Directory Co., 1899.

Hursch, Simon. Clinton, Henry County, Missouri, United States Census, 1880, sheet 358C.

The Insurance Year Book 1918-1919: Life, Casualty and Miscellaneous Corrected to June 20, 1918. New York: Spectator Co., 1918.

Jacobs, Joseph. "Jewish Population of the United States Memoir of the Bureau of Jewish Statistics of the American Jewish Committee." *Jewish American Yearbook*, Vol. 16. Philadelphia: Jewish Publication Society of America, 1914. 341346.

"Jewish National Organizations in the United States." *American Jewish Year Book*, Vol. 16 Philadelphia: Jewish Publication Society, 1914-1915.

Jewish Statistics." *American Jewish Year Book*, Vol. 5. Philadelphia: Jewish Publication Society, 1903. 143-146.

Kertzer, Morris N. "Religion." *American Jewish Year Book*, Vol. 53. Philadelphia: Jewish Pub. Society, 1952. 154-165.

Karchmer, Benj. Springfield Ward 2, Greene, Missouri, United States Census, 1920, sheet 2B.

Karchmer, Benjamin. Springfield, Greene, Missouri, United States Census, 1930, sheet 2B.

Kemp, Morris. Borough of Manhattan, New York City, Ward 8, New York County, New York, United States Census 1900, sheet 21A.

Kohen, Julius. Cincinnati, United States Census, 1880, sheet 26.

Kransberg, Fred. Springfield Ward 5, Greene, Missouri, United States Census, 1920, sheet 2B.

Kranzberg, Edward. Tract SLC39, Olivette Clayton Township, St. Louis, Missouri, United States Census, 1940, sheet 10B.

Kranzberg, Jake. St. Louis Ward 5, St. Louis (Independent City), Missouri, United States Census, 1910, sheet 13B.

____. Springfield Ward 1, Greene, Missouri, United States Census, 1920, sheet 11A.

Lebolt, Charles. Pique, Miami, Ohio, United States Census, 1880, sheet 295C.

Levy, Moses. Missouri. United States Census, 1900, sheet 21A.

____. Saxonia records. 14 June 1864. "United States Germans to America Index, 1850-1897." Accessed February 8, 2015. familysearch. org/ark:/61903/1:1:KDQL-5C1.

Levy, Sylvain. Springfield, Missouri. United States Census, 1870, p. 64.

Linfield, Harry S. "Statistics of Jews." *American Jewish Year Book*, Vol. 24. Philadelphia: Jewish Publication Society, 1922. 298-322.

____. "Statistics of Jews." *American Jewish Year Book*, Vol. 25. Philadelphia: Jewish Publication Society, 1923. 325-364.

"Local Organizations." *American Jewish Year Book*, Vol. 21. Philadelphia: Jewish Publication Society, 1919. 330-583.

Levy, Sylvaian. Litchfield, Montgomery, Illinois. United States Census, 1880, sheet 389C.

Marx, Jake. Central Township, Missouri. United States Census, 1880, sheet 194D.

Mendel, Moses. Hot Springs Township, Hot Springs city Ward 3, Garland, Arkansas, United States Census, 1900, sheet 8A.

"Missouri Population 1900-1990." Missouri Census Data Center March 31, 2014, 17.

Moakowitz, Morris. St. Louis, Ward 20, St. Louis (Independent City), Missouri,

United States Census, 1910, sheet 14A.

Moskowitz, Morris. Borough of Brooklyn, City of New York, Kings County, New York, United States Census, 1900, sheet 237A.

Netter, Marx. Campbell, Greene County, Missouri. United States Census, 1920, sheet 3A.

____. Campbell Township, Greene County, Missouri, United States Census, 1930, sheet 4B.

Nathan, B.S.C. Township Greenfield city Ward 1-2, Dade, Missouri, United States Census, 1900, sheet 4A.

1905 Springfield, Missouri City Directory. Accessed February 4, 2015, www.greenecountymo.org/archives/1905_city_directory.php.

"1938 Directory of Jewish Federations, Welfare Funds and Community Councils." *American Jewish Year Book*, Vol. 40. Philadelphia: Jewish Publication Society, 1939. 481-516.

Preliminary Report: 1988 Congregational Survey. Springfield, MO: United Hebrew Congregations, 1988. OJA.

Rothschild, Jacob. Campbell Township Springfield city Ward 2, Greene, Missouri, United States Census, 1900, sheet 31B.

Rubenstien, Joseph F. Center Township Greenfield city Ward 1-2, Dade, Missouri, United States Census, sheet 10B.

Samors, Harry. Springfield, Ward 4, Greene, Missouri, United States Census 1920, sheet 6A.

Scharff, Dan. Springfield, Greene, Missouri, United States Census, 1930, sheet 12B.

Scharff, Daniel. Mississippi, Census, 1870, p. 264.

Schorff, Maxiamial. Campbell Township, Springfield, City Ward 2, Greene, Missouri, United States Census, 1900, sheet 19B.

Scharff, Nathan. Jackson Township, Greene, Missouri. United States Census, 1920.

Schwab, David. Springfield, Greene, Missouri, United States Census, 1930, sheet 4B.

____. Springfield, Ward I, Springfield, Campbell Township, Greene, Missouri, United States Census, 1940, sheet 19B.

Schwab, Max. Springfield, Greene, Missouri, United States Census, 1930, sheet 5B.

Seligman, Ben B. "Changes in the Jewish Population in the United States." *American Jewish Year Book*, Vol. 52. Philadelphia: Jewish Publication Society, 1951. 3-20.

Seligman, Ben B. and Alvin Chenkin. "Jewish Population of the United

States, 1953." *American Jewish Year Book*, Vol. 54. Philadelphia: Jewish Publication Society, 1951. 3-12.

Somers, Victor. Missouri, United States Census, 1870, p. 46.

"Springfield Petitions, Name Index to Naturalization Petitions ca. 1911 ca. 1983." National Archives at Kansas City. 28 September 2012 Accessed April 21, 2015. www.archives.gov/kansas-city/finding-aids/naturalization-springfield.html.

"Statistics of Jews." *American Jewish Year Book*, Vol. 17. Philadelphia: Jewish Publication Society, 1915. 343-355.

"Statistics of Jews." *American Jewish Year Book*, Vol. 18. Philadelphia: Jewish Publication Society, 1916. 275-287.

"Statistics of Jews." *American Jewish Year Book*, Vol. 19. Philadelphia: Jewish Publication Society, 1918. 409-433.

"Statistics of Jews," *American Jewish Year Book*, Vol. 1. Philadelphia: Jewish Publication Society, 1922. 298-322.

Summers, Victor. Center, Greene County, Missouri, United States Census 1880, sheet 199A.

Sussman, Benjamin. Brooklyn Assembly District 4, Kings, New York, United States Census, 1920, sheet 8B.

Sussman, Bennie. Springfield, Greene County, Missouri, United States Census, 1930, sheet 21A.

Sussman, Mike. Springfield Ward 1, Greene County, Missouri, United States census, 1920, sheet 1B.

"Total Population by County, 1900-2000." Missouri Census Data Center. March 31, 2014.

Wallerstein, Hermon. Virginia, United States Census, 1870, p. 172.

Wasserman, Samuel S. Peoria Ward 4, Peoria, Illinois, United States Census, 1910, sheet 3A.

Weigle, Guttman and Katie Trawer. Marriage License, St. Louis, Missouri, July 22, 1883.

Wennerman, Jake. Springfield Ward 1, Greene County, Missouri, United States Census, 1920, sheet 8B.

Winnerman, Abe. St Louis Ward 28, St Louis (Independent City), MO, United States Census, 1920, sheet 5A.

Winnerman. Abraham. Stilwell Ward 1, Adair County, Oklahoma, United States Census, 1910, sheet 2B.

Wygle, George. Springfield, Missouri. United States Census, 1910. District 26, sheet 5B.

Wigle, George. Springfield, Missouri. United States Census, 1900. District 39, sheet 11A.

Histories

Abrams, Jeanne E. *Jewish Women Pioneering the Frontier Trail: A History in the American West*. New York: New York University Press, 2006.

Barlow, Mary L. *The Why of Fort Scott*. n.p.: n.p., 1921.

"Ben Hirschland." *The Story of Oklahoma City Oklahoma*. Vol. 3. Chicago: S. J. Clarke Pub., 1912.

Blevins, Brooks. *A History of the Ozarks: The Conflicted Ozarks*, Vol. 2. Urbana: University of Illinois Press, 2019.

Crockett, Norman L. "A Study in Confusion: Missouri's Immigration Program, 1865-1916," *Missouri Historical Review* 57 (April 1963): 248-260.

Croly, Jane Cunningham. *The history of the woman's club movement in America*. New York: Henry G. Allen & Co., 1989.

Cutler, William B. "Bourbon County; Part 14." *History of the State of Kansas*. Chicago: A.T. Andreas, 1883.

Diner, Hasia. "Entering the Mainstream of Modern Jewish History: Peddlers and the American Jewish South." *Southern Jewish History* 8 (2005): 1–30.

____. *A Time for Gathering: The Second Migration 1820-1880*. Baltimore: Johns Hopkins University Press, 1992.

Dorsey, G. Volney. "Washington Township and the City of Piqua." *The 1880 History of Miami County Ohio*. n.p.: n.p., 1880.

"Dying in America: A Chronology." A Family Undertaking. Public Broadcasting Station, August 3, 2004. Accessed May 15, 2015. www.pbs. org/pov/afamilyundertaking/photo_gallery_special_death. php#. VgAlaZf0c6E.

Ehrlich, Walter. *Zion in the Valley: The Jewish Community of St. Louis*. Vol. 1. 1807-1907. Columbia: University of Missouri Press, 1997.

Ely, Carol. *Jewish Louisville: Portrait of a Community*. Louisville: Jewish Community Federation of Louisville, 2003.

Fairbanks, Jonathan and Clyde Edwin Tuck. *Past and Present of Greene County, Missouri*. n.p.: n.p., 1914.

"Find a Garden." American Community Gardening Association. n.d. Community Garden. Accessed May 18, 2015. communitygarden.org/find-a-garden/gardens/temple-israel-community-garden/?back=https%3A%2F%2Fcommunitygarden.org%2Ffind-a-garden%2F.

"The First Bat Mitzvah in the United States." *Jewish Virtual Library*, 2015.

Accessed June 6, 2015. www.jewishvirtuallibrary.org/jsource/ Judaism/ firstbat.html.

"Fort Smith Congregations." *Encyclopedia of Southern Jewish Communities*, Goldring/Woldenberg Institute of Southern Jewish Life, 2015. Accessed April 13, 2015. www.isjl.org/arkansas-fort-smith-congregations-encyclopedia.html.

"Freshman." *Souwester*. Springfield, Missouri: Drury College, 1916.

Gartner, Lloyd P. "American Judaism, 1880-1945." In *The Cambridge Companion to American Judaism*. Edited by Dana Evan Kaplan. New York: Cambridge University Press, 2005. 43-60.

Glazer, Nathan. *American Judaism*. Chicago: University of Chicago Press, 1957.

Goodspeed. *Pictorial and Genealogical Record of Greene County, Missouri*. n.p.: n.p. 1893.

"Henry S. Jacobs Camp, Utica." *Encyclopedia of Southern Jewish Communities*, 2015. Accessed April 13, 2015. www.isjl.org/mississippi-utica-encyclopedia.html.

Hertzberg, Arthur. *The Jews in America: Four Centuries of an Uneasy Encounter: A History*. New York: Simon and Schuster, 1989.

"History." *American Legion*. n.d. Accessed July 21, 2015. www.legion. org/history.

"History." *Chesed Shel Emeth Society*. n.d. Accessed July 7, 2015. www. chesedshelemeth.org/history.html.

"History." *Hadassah*. Hadassah, the Women's Zionist Organization of America, 2015. Accessed July 11, 2015. www.hadassah.org/about/ history. html?referrer.

"History." *The Shrine Mosque*, n.d. Accessed May 11, 2015. www.theshrinemosqueonline.com/history.

"History." *Union for Reform Judaism*. 2015. Accessed February 18, 2015. urj.org/about/union/history/.

A History of the Department of Chemistry and Chemical Engineering of Lehigh University (1866-1941). Bethlehem, PA: Lehigh University, n.d.

"History of Nevada/Vernon County" Chamber of Commerce: Nevada, MO, Vernon County. 2015. Accessed February 8, 2015. www.nevada-mo.com/ page/10354_2.

The History of Pettis County, Missouri, including an authentic history of Sedalia, and other towns and Township. n.p: n.p., 1882.

A History of the Jews of Louisville, KY. New Orleans, LA: Jewish Historical Society, 1900.

Holcombe, Ira ed., *History of Greene County, Missouri*. St. Louis, MO: Western Historical Co., 1883.

Hruschka, John. *How Books Came to America: The Rise of the American Book Trade*. University Park: Penn State University Press, 2012.

Hubble, Janie. Report of Historian for the Ladies for year 1935-1936. Ladies Saturday Club. History Museum on the Square, Springfield, MO.

Jacob, Ernest Israel. "Fifty Years of Jewish Life in Springfield, MO." *Fifty Years: Temple Israel, Springfield, MO*. Springfield, MO: Temple Israel, November 19, 1943.

____. "Installation in Springfield." Temple Israel, Springfield, MO. 1942. Reprint in *Paths of Faithfulness: A Collection of Sermons by Ernest I. Jacob*. Edited by Walter Jacob and Herbert Jacob. Pittsburgh, PA: n.p., 1964. 1-3.

____. Summary of the History of the Jews of Springfield. n.p.: Springfield, MO, n.d. Manuscript. OJA.

Jacob, Herbert. "The Rabbi's Role in a Midwestern Community." In *Paths of Faithfulness: A Collection of Sermons by Ernest I. Jacob*. Edited by Walter Jacob and Herbert Jacob. Pittsburgh, PA: n.p., 1964. xxix-xxxvi.

Landau, Herman. Adath Louisville: *The Story of the Jewish Community*. Louisville, KY: Herman Landau and Associates, 1981.

Leonard, John W. *The Book of St. Louisans*. St. Louis: St. Louis, MO Republic, 1906.

Levy, Louis Edward. "The Russian Jewish Refugees in America." Board of Presidents of the National Societies of Philadelphia, Philadelphia, PA. 1891. Reprint in *The American Jew as Patriot, Soldier and Citizen*. Edited by Simon Wolf. Cranbury, NJ: Scholar's Bookshelf, 2006. 544.

Marblestone, David. *Samuel Cohen and Augusta Spiro Levy and Their Families*. Chevy Chase, MD: David Marblestone, January 11, 2004.

Marcus, Jacob Rader. "The American Colonial Jew: A Study in Acculturation." In *The American Jewish Experience*. Edited by Jonathan D. Sarna. New York: Holmes & Meier, 1986. 6-19.

____. *United States Jewry 1776-1985*. Vol. 3. Detroit, MI: Wayne State University Press, 1993.

Mansberg, Danny and Linda Orlansky Posner. "New HSJ Director Announced." Jacobs Camp, May 19, 2015. blogs.rj.org/jacobs/2014/05/19/great-news-from-the-henry-s-jacobs-camp-committee/.

McIntyre, Stephen. "'The City Belongs to the Local Unions': The Rise of the Springfield Labor Movement, 1871-1912," *Missouri Historical Review* 98 (October 2003): 24-46.

Members of the Springfield Ladies Saturday Club. 1878. Ladies Saturday Club.

THMOTS.

Meyer, Michael A. "German-Jewish Identity in Nineteenth-Century America." In *The American Jewish Experience*. Edited by Jonathan D. Sarna. New York: Holmes & Meier, 1986. 45–61.

____. "Thank You, Moritz Loth: A 125-Year UAHC Retrospective." *Reform Judaism* (Fall 1998): 31.

Minutes of Last Man's Club, 1940. American Legion Post 69, Springfield, MO.

"Mission." *Council of Churches of the Ozarks*. Facebook, n.d. Accessed July 27, 2015.

"Mission." *Hadassah*. Hadassah, the Women's Zionist Organization of America, 2015. Accessed July 11, 2015. www.hadassah.org/about/.

"Missouri." *Gazetteer and Business Directory Cities and Towns*, 16. n.p.: n.p., 1881.

"Orders to Officers of the Medical Corps, U.S. Army." *Journal of the American Medical Association* 72 (1919): 735.

Piehl, Charles K. "The Race of Improvement: Springfield Society 1865-1881." In *The Ozarks in Missouri History: Discoveries in an American Region*. Edited by Lynn Morrow, 71-100. Columbia: University of Missouri Press, 2013.

"Pine Bluff, Arkansas." *Encyclopedia of Southern Jewish Communities*, 2014. Accessed August 25, 2011. www.isjl.org/arkansas-pine-bluff-encyclopedia. html.

"Post 69 Springfield, MO, Missouri." *The American Legion Centennial Celebration*. n.d. Accessed July 21, 2015. centennial.legion.org/missouri/ post69.

Postal, Bernard. "B'nai Brith: A Century of Service." *American Jewish Year Book*, Vol. 15, 97-116. Philadelphia: Jewish Publication Society, 1914.

Prince, Benjamin, ed. *A Standard History of Springfield and Clark County, Ohio*, Vol. 2. Chicago: American Historical Society, 1922.

"Residences and Flats." Western Contractor 14 January 1914: 32.

Scopes, John Thomas. *The World's Most Famous Court Trial: Tennessee Evolution Case: A Complete stenographic report of the Tennessee Anti-Evolution Act, At Dayton, July 10 to 21, 1925. Including speeches and arguments of attorneys*. National Book: Cincinnati, OH, 1925.

Shepard, E.M. "Chapter XVIII: Women's Club." In *Past and Present of Greene County, Missouri Early and Recent History and Genealogical Records of Many of the Representative Citizens*, 561. Edited by Jonathan Fairbanks and Clyde Edwin Tuck. n.p.: n.p., 1914.

Sherwin, Byron. In *Partnership with God*. New York: Syracuse University Press, 1990.

Shevitz, Amy Hill. *Jewish Communities on the Ohio River: A History*. Lexington: University Press of Kentucky, 2007.

"The Shrine Mosque History & Preservation Association." *The Shrine Mosque.* n.d. Accessed June 23, 2015. www.abashrine.com/ shrine-mosque-history---preservation.html.

Silverstein, Alan. *Alternatives to Assimilation: The Response of Reform Judaism to American Culture, 1840-1930*. Hanover, NH: Brandeis University Press, 1994.

Skrabec, Quentin R. Jr., "1882—Recession." In *The 100 Most Important American Financial Crises: An Encyclopedia of the Lowest Points in American Economic History*, Santa Barbara, CA: Greenwood, 2005. 101-102.

Smith, M. C. "Chapter 17: Secret Societies." In *Past and Present of Greene County, Missouri*. n.p.: n.p., 1914.

Spalding's Official Base Ball Guide for 1905-06. New York: American Sports Publishing Company, 1905

Stevens, Albert C. ed. *The Cyclopedia of Fraternities*. New York: Hamilton Printing, 1899.

Stevens, Walter Barlow. *Missouri the Center State 1821-1915*, Vol. 3. St. Louis: S. J. Clarke Publishing, 1915.

Thoburn, Joseph B. and Muriel H. Wright. "Julius Bookman," in *Oklahoma, A History of the State and its People*, Vol. 3, 139. New York: Lewis Historical Publishing Company, 1929.

Weissbach, Lee Shai. "Decline in an Age of Expansion: Disappearing Jewish Communities in the Era of Mass Migration." *American Jewish Archives Journal* 42 (1997): 39-61.

____. "East European Immigrants and the Image of Jews in the SmallTown South." *American Jewish History* 85 (September 1997): 231–262.

____. *Jewish Life in Small-Town America: A History*. New Haven: Yale University Press, 2005.

Legal Documents

Aetschults, Isaac and Bertha LeBolt. Marriage License. Miami, Ohio, June 25, 1884.

Breadman, Birth Certificate. Chicago, Cook, Illinois, December 31, 1923.

Breadman, Ida. Death Certificate. Missouri, January 12, 1931.

Brownlow, Elizabeth. Death Certificate. July 15, 1938. Cook County, Illinois. "Illinois, Cook County Deaths, 1878-1939, 1955-1994."

Cohen, Isaac and Hannah Lorber. Marriage License. Whitely, Indiana.

January 19, 1896.

Cohen, Pauline. Birth Certificate. Kansas City, MO. April 8, 1904.

"Deed Records 1833-1877." Greene County, Missouri Listing of Buyers and Sellers of Property 1833-1877. Accessed October 21, 2015. www.greenecountymo.org/archives/deed_records.php.

Diamond, Bruce and United Hebrew Congregations. Contract. August 1, 1989. OJA.

Flanders, Robert. Netter-Ullman Building. National Register of Historic Places Registration. United States Department of the Interior National Park Service Form. February 2003.

Fox, Carrie. Death Certificate. Cincinnati, Ohio. February 15, 1933.

Hirsch, Adolph H. Death Certificate. El Paso, Texas. March 30, 1949.

Hirschland, Benjamin and Leonara Riegelman. Marriage License. Des Moine, Iowa. October 14, 1890.

Lesueur, Alexander. Official Manual of the State of Missouri for the Years 1893-94. Jefferson City: Tribune Printing, 1893.

Karchmer, Benjamin. Death Certificate. Springfield, MO. May 27, 1954.

Karchmer, Jennie. Death Certificate. Springfield, Missouri. April 22, 1943.

Kemp, Samuel. Birth Certificate. New York, New York, February 27, 1883.

____. Draft Registration. Springfield, MO. 1917-1918.

Kemp, Samuel Sidney and Eura Kemp. Divorce Decree. Springfield, MO. May 16, 1919. Springfield, MO: Greene County Missouri Circuit Court Divorces, n.d. 155.

Kranzberg, Edward. Draft Registration. Springfield, MO. 1917-1918.

Kranzberg, Jake. Draft Registration. Springfield, MO. 1917-1918.

Kranzberg, Morris and Pauline Betty Lopin. Marriage License. Vigo, IN. December 16, 1946

Levy, David and Henriette Rosenheim. Marriage License. New York, NY, September 10, 1873.

Levy, Moses and Henriette Levy. Marriage License. New York, NY, August 30, 1887.

Lotven, Israel Mitchell. Draft Registration. Springfield, MO 1917-1918.

Marx, Jake and Frances Cohn. Marriage License. Louisville, KY, 1877.

Moskowitz, Ben. Death Certificate. Springfield, MO, January 23, 1930.

Moskowitz, Hannah. Death Certificate. St. Louis, Missouri: August 21, 1917.

Moskowitz, Morris. Death Certificate. St. Louis, MO, September 27, 1920.

Netter, Marx and Fay Scharff. Marriage License. Springfield, MO. July 6, 1910.

"Note." 17 January 1906. Minute Book, 1906-1916. Willard, MO: Bank of Willard, 1906-1916.

Oppenheimer vs. Sommers. In *Southwestern Reporter*, Vol. 19,
    St. Paul: West Publishing, 1892. 711-712.

Scharff, M. and Rosa Scharff. Marriage License. Adams, MS, September 6,
    1882.

Scharff, Max. Silesia Passenger Manifest. August 28, 1872. Accessed March 5,
    2015. familysearch.org/pal:/MM9.1.1/KDWC-XVX.

Scharff, Max and Carrie Hart. Marriage License. Hamilton, OH.
    September 1, 1895.

Schwab, Irving and Ben Karchmer. Agreement. Temple Israel and Sha'are
    Zedek. Springfield, MO. October 16, 1946.

Schwab, Max and Lena Zeigler. Marriage License. Huntington, WV,
    January 1, 1896.

Sommer, Victor. Marriage License. Louisville, KY, March 26, 1869.

Sussman, Ben. Death Certificate. Springfield, MO. May 16, 1941.

Sussman, Mike. Draft Registration, Springfield, MO, 1917.

Ullman, Lee. Draft Registration card. Springfield, MO. September 12, 1918.

Ullman, Ludwig. Death Certificate. Springfield, MO. June 30, 1910.

Ullman, Samson and Sarah Wallerstein. Marriage license. Richmond, VA.
    October 13, 1853.

Wallerstein, Catherin Sara. Birth certificate. Richmond, VA. November 18, 1892.

Wallerstein, Clara Ullman. Passport. May 2, 1922.

Wallerstein, Mortan Ludwig. Birth certificate. Richmond, VA. December 7,
    1890.

Wennerman, Jacob. Death Certificate. MO. March 2, 1920.

Wennerman, Mary. Death Certificate. MO, June 15, 1923.

Winnerman, Abe and Fannie Winnerman. Marriage License. Springfield, MO,
    February 7, 1900.

Winnerman, Abraham and Fannie Lobilsky. Marriage License. St. Louis, MO,
    January 1, 1887.

Winnerman, Abraham and Fannie Winnerman. Divorce Decree #29064.
    Greene County, Missouri Circuit Court. September 14, 1899.

Winnerman, Fannie. Testimony. Queens, State of New York, April 2, 1941.

Winnerman, Fannie and A. Winnerman. Divorce Decree #30196. Greene
    County, Missouri Circuit Court, September 13, 1900.

Organizational Documents

Annual Congregational Meeting Minutes. United Hebrew Congregations.
    Springfield, MO. February 19, 1989. OJA.

Armstrong, Anglus. Minutes of Last Man's Club. November 1934. American Legion Post 69, Springfield, MO.

Articles of Association. Springfield, MO: Share [*sic*] Zedek. December 21, 1918.

Articles of Association. Springfield, MO: Temple Israel, November 4, 1893.

B'nai Brith Cash Book. Springfield, MO. 1912-1973. OJA.

B'nai Brith Minutes Book. Springfield, MO. 1926-1962. OJA.

Board Meeting. United Hebrew Congregations. Springfield, MO. Minutes. n.d. OJA.

Board Meeting. United Hebrew Congregations. Springfield, MO. Minutes. June 29, 1970. OJA.

Board Meeting. United Hebrew Congregations. Springfield, MO. October 7, 1971. OJA.

Board Meeting. United Hebrew Congregations. Springfield, MO. June 5, 1972. OJA.

Board Meeting. United Hebrew Congregations. Springfield, MO. August 14, 1972. OJA.

Board Meeting. United Hebrew Congregations. Springfield, MO. November 22, 1972. OJA.

Board Meeting. United Hebrew Congregations. Springfield, MO. February 19, 1973. OJA.

Board Meeting. United Hebrew Congregations. Springfield, MO. June 19, 1973. OJA.

Board Meeting. United Hebrew Congregations. Springfield, MO. August 28, 1973. OJA.

Board Meeting. United Hebrew Congregations. Springfield, MO. December 26, 1973. OJA.

Board Meeting. United Hebrew Congregations. Springfield, MO. January 14, 1975. OJA.

Board Meeting. United Hebrew Congregations. Springfield, MO. June 30, 1975. OJA.

Board Meeting. United Hebrew Congregations. Springfield, MO. August 29, 1974. OJA.

Board Meeting. United Hebrew Congregations. Springfield, MO. July 21, 1976. OJA.

Board Meeting. United Hebrew Congregations. Springfield, MO. February 21, 1978. OJA.

Board Meeting. United Hebrew Congregations. Springfield, MO. March 5, 1978. OJA.

Board Meeting. United Hebrew Congregations. Springfield, MO.
April 18, 1980. OJA.

Board Meeting. United Hebrew Congregations. Springfield, MO.
October 9, 1980. OJA.

Board Meeting. United Hebrew Congregations. Springfield, MO.
February 21, 1982. OJA.

Board Meeting. United Hebrew Congregations. Springfield, MO.
February 13, 1983. OJA.

Board Meeting. United Hebrew Congregations. Springfield, MO.
February 27, 1985. OJA.

Board Meeting. United Hebrew Congregations. Springfield, MO.
April 24, 1985. OJA.

Board Meeting. United Hebrew Congregations. Springfield, MO.
May 29, 1985. OJA.

Board Meeting. United Hebrew Congregations. Springfield, MO.
August 28, 1985. OJA.

Board Meeting. United Hebrew Congregations. Springfield, MO.
June 24, 1986. OJA.

Board Meeting. United Hebrew Congregations. Springfield, MO.
September 7, 1986. OJA.

Board Meeting. United Hebrew Congregations. Springfield, MO.
October 26, 1986. OJA.

Board Meeting. United Hebrew Congregations. Springfield, MO.
February 15, 1987. OJA.

Board Meeting. United Hebrew Congregations. Springfield, MO.
May 17, 1987. OJA.

Board Meeting. United Hebrew Congregations. Springfield, MO.
September 27, 1987. OJA.

Board Meeting. United Hebrew Congregations. Springfield, MO.
October 25, 1987. OJA.

Board Meeting. United Hebrew Congregations. Springfield, MO.
January 12, 1988. OJA.

Board Meeting. United Hebrew Congregations. Springfield, MO.
August 24 1989. OJA.

Board Meeting. United Hebrew Congregations. Temple Israel, Springfield,
MO. February 10, 1998. OJA.

Board Meeting. United Hebrew Congregations. Springfield, MO.
July 26, 1988. OJA.

Board Meeting. United Hebrew Congregations. Springfield, MO. October 30, 1988. OJA.

Board Meeting. United Hebrew Congregations. Springfield, MO. September 21, 1989. OJA.

Board Meeting. United Hebrew Congregations. Springfield, MO. October 22, 1989. OJA.

Board Meeting. United Hebrew Congregations. Springfield, MO. December 17, 1989. OJA.

Board Meeting. United Hebrew Congregations. Springfield, MO. November 11, 1997. OJA.

Board Meeting. United Hebrew Congregations. Springfield, MO. September 1, 1998. OJA.

Board Meeting. Temple Israel. Springfield, Missouri. Minutes. August 24, 1999. OJA.

Board Meeting. United Hebrew Congregations. Springfield, MO. August 19, 2001. OJA.

Board Meeting. United Hebrew Congregations. Springfield, MO. March 13, 2005. OJA.

Board Meeting. United Hebrew Congregations. Springfield, MO. April 15, 2005. OJA.

Board Meeting. United Hebrew Congregations. Springfield, MO. June 11, 2006. OJA.

Boy Scouts of America. Tenth Annual Report. April 9, 1920. OJA.

Building Committee. United Hebrew Congregations. Report. February 19, 1989. OJA.

Business Meetings Book. Ladies Aid Society. 1924-1933. OJA.

Cemetery Rules. Springfield, Missouri: United Hebrew Congregations, c.1985. OJA.

Central Conference of American Rabbis. Resolution on Same Gender Officiation. CCAR, March 2000. www.ccarnet. org/rabbis-speak/ resolutions/2000/same-gender-officiation/. Accessed 6 June 2015.

Chapter Founding Dates [of Hadassah Chapters]. n.d. American Jewish Historical Society.

Chapter of Hadassah, Springfield, MO Minutes. 1986-1989. OJA.

Chapter 227 State Highway System. Missouri Revised Statutes. August 28, 2013. Sec. 227.410.

Claflin et al. v. Sommers. St. Louis Court of Appeals. February 18, 1890. In *Cases Determined in the St. Louis and the Kansas City Courts of Appeals of the State of Missouri from January 6, 1890, to March 18, 1890*, Vol. 39, 419-

424. Columbia, MO: E. W. Stephens, 1890.

"Classified List of Members." *Thirty-third Annual Report of the Union of American Hebrew Congregations.* Cincinnati, OH: May & Kreidler, June 12, 1904. 5832.

"Community Garden, Temple Israel." Religious Action Center of Reform Judaism. Reform Judaism, March 23, 2009. Accessed May 15, 2015. resources.rj.org/Articles/index.cfm?id=1393.

"Company Overview." *Council of Churches of the Ozarks.* Facebook. n.d. Accessed July 27, 2015.

"Complete Death Register from 1850 to Present." New Mt. Sinai Cemetery. 2015. www.newmtsinaicemetery. org/death_register.asp. Accessed February 3, 2015.

Congregational Meeting. United Hebrew Congregations, Springfield, MO. March 9, 1980. OJA.

Congregational Meeting. United Hebrew Congregations, Springfield, MO. March 8, 1981. OJA.

Congregational Meeting. Temple Israel, Springfield, MO. April 19, 1998. OJA.

Congregational Meeting. Temple Israel, Springfield, MO. April 18, 1999. OJA.

Congregational Meeting. Temple Israel, Springfield, MO. April 16, 2000. OJA.

Congregational Meeting. Temple Israel, Springfield, MO. April 7, 2001. OJA.

Congregational Meeting. Temple Israel, Springfield, MO. April 20, 2003. OJA.

Constitution and By-laws of the Springfield Ladies Saturday Club as Amended. Springfield, MO: Charles Nevatt, 1890.

"Copy of Agreement." *Springfield Missouri Republican,* December 1, 1907, p. 16.

Cornerstone. Temple Israel, Springfield, MO, now Rogersville, MO. 1930.

Crawford, A. B. et al. *v.* Boston Store Mercantile Company et al. St. Louis Court of Appeals, May 19, 1898. In *Cases Determined by the St. Louis and the Kansas City Courts of Appeals of the State of Missouri, from May 19, 1896, to December 8, 1896,* Vol. 67. Columbia, MO: E. W. Stephens Publishing, 1897. 40-41.

"Fain Awards: FAQs." *Religious Action Center of Reform Judaism.* Reform Judaism, 2015. Accessed May 15, 2015. www.rac.org/fain-awards-faqs.

Future Planning Committee. Annual Report. February 29, 1988. OJA.

House & Building Rules. Temple Israel, Springfield, MO. November 12, 1979. OJA.

Independent Order of Odd Fellows. Springfield Lodge No. 218 (Springfield, Missouri). 1884-1939. R 614. The State Historical Society of Missouri Manuscript Collection. Springfield, MO.

Kramer, Robert C., et al. Special Committee to evaluate the Constitution and By-Laws. April 1, 1976. OJA.

Level, Dorsey E. "Thank You." 1 April 1995. Certificate. Private Collection.

Proceedings of the District Grand Lodge 2, B'nai Brith. April 1912. Records of B'nai Brith International, American Jewish Archives, Cincinnati, OH.

Programme of the Springfield Ladies Saturday Club for 1891-1892. Springfield, Missouri: Charles Nevatt, 1891. Ladies Saturday Club. THMOTS.

Schwartz, Howard. Annual Dues and Membership Committee Report. February 10, 1985. OJA.

Service of Installation for Rabbi H.D. Uriel Smith. Springfield, Missouri: United Hebrew Congregations, August 25, 1972. OJA.

Sha'are Zedek Congregation. 1918-1943. Plaque. Temple Israel, Rogersville, Missouri.

Sherwin, Rita Report to the Annual Congregational Meeting. Temple Israel, Springfield, MO. April 29, 2007. OJA.

Special Meeting of Union of Hebrew Congregations Members. Temple Israel, Springfield, MO, May 23, 1982. OJA.

Strauss, Lester. Report of the President of Temple Israel. September 28, 1941. OJA.

____. Report of the President of the Temple Israel. September 20, 1942. OJA.

Temple Israel Board Minutes. Springfield, Missouri: Temple Israel, 1914-1960. OJA.

Temple Israel 1893-1943. Plaque. Temple Israel, Rogersville, Missouri.

Temple Israel Kitchen & Food. Springfield, MO: Temple Israel, November 14, 1995. OJA. Treasury Book. Sisterhood of Temple Israel. 1988-2000. OJA.

Twenty-fifth anniversary of the first graduation from the Hebrew Union College. Cincinnati, OH: Hebrew Union College Press, 1908.

"Supporting Interfaith." Union for Reform Judaism 2015. Accessed June 6, 2015. urj.org/cong/outreach/interfaith/.

Yearly Membership Meeting. Temple Israel, Springfield, MO. February 8, 1970, p. 2. OJA.

Periodicals

417 Magazine

Davis, Julie Sedenko. "History Gets a Facelift." *417 Magazine*, February 2013. www.417mag.com/417-Magazone/February-2013/Hotel-Van-divort-Springfield-MO/.

American Hatter
"St. Louis and the Southwest." *American Hatter*, August 1909.

American Israelite
Lefkowitz, David. "The Duty of the Home." *American Israelite*, April 12, 1917.

American Negro
The Old Reliable Advertisement. *American Negro*, October 25, 1890.

Army and Navy Gazette
Townsend, E. D. "Absent without leave." *Army and Navy Official Gazette* 1 (1864).

Bartlett Times
"Father of Mrs. I Gold Dies Monday in Taylor." *Bartlett Times* [Texas],
    July 7, 1933.
Bias Bias, May 5, 1953: Front Cover. THMOTS.
Billings, Jim. "Citizen of the Year." *Bias,* December 29, 1952. THMOTS.
"A Gift for Edith." *Bias,* August 4, 1954. THMOTS.
"On the Bias." *Bias,* August 10, 1954. THMOTS.
Strainchamps, Ethel. "Citizen of the Week." Bias, October 10, 1951. THMOTS.
"Talk of the Town." *Bias,* December 22, 1953. THMOTS.
"Town Talk." *Bias,* June 15, 1954. THMOTS.
Windle, Jewell E. "Have We Been Away." *Bias,* March 3, 1953. THMOTS.

Boot and Shoe Recorder
"Interesting Items." *Boot and Shoe Recorder*, July 3, 1901.

Bottles and Extras
Sullivan, Jack. "'Small Sam' Altschul and his Tall Tale." *Bottles and Extras,*
    November-December 2010.

Chronicle
"Death of Mrs. Marx Netter." *Chronicle*, April 10, 1908.
"Fayette, two petitions for liquor license renewal." *Chronicle*, February 20,
    1903. jeffersoncountyms.org/Newspapers/100yearsago.htm.
    Accessed March 19, 2015.

Clothier and Furnisher
"Cincinnati." *Clothier and Furnisher*, July 1895.
"Clothing and Furnishing Notes." *Clothier and Furnisher*, March 1895.

Courier-Journal
"Mrs. Dora Backrow Dead." *Courier-Journal*, May 19, 1898.

Dallas Daily Times Herald
"An Object of Interest." *Dallas Daily Times Herald*, December 17, 1892.

Daily Leader
Star Clothing House Advertisement. *Daily Leader* 1870.

Daily News
"Funeral, at 3 Today." *Daily News*, December 3, 1931, morning ed.
"Mrs. Dan Scharff Dies at her Home." *Daily News*, January 27, 1933, morning ed.

Engineering and Contracting
"Buildings." *Engineering and Contracting*, February 21, 1912.

Fort Scott Monitor
"Mr. Sam Cohen." *Fort Scott Monitor*, April 29, 1880.

Greenfield Vidette
"N. B. Nathan," *Greenfield Vidette*, February 18, 1932.

Herald
"Mrs. Emmanuel Mars." *Herald*, September 27, 1887. In *Abstracts of Items of
    Genealogical Interest from the Springfield, Greene County, MO newspapers
    for 1887 and 1884*. Edited by William K. Hall. St. Louis: n.p., 1993. 102.
"Mr. Ferd. Bakrow." *Herald*, July 12, 1883, morning ed. In *Abstracts of Items of
    Genealogical Interest from the Springfield, Greene County,*
MO newspapers for 1883 and 1884. Edited by William K. Hall. St. Louis: n.p.,
    1994. 32.
"Son born." *Herald*, January 7, 1886, morning ed. In *Abstracts of Items of
    Genealogical Interest from the Springfield, Greene County, MO news-papers
    for 1886*. Edited by William K. Hall. St. Louis: n.p., 1993. 2.

JAMA
"Deaths." *JAMA* 55 (July 23, 1910).
"Deaths." *JAMA* 68 (June 23, 1917).

Jefferson City Post-Tribune
"Noon and Afternoon." *Jefferson City Post-Tribune*, September 20, 1932.

Leader
"Altschul Funeral to be Held Next Sunday." *Leader*, evening ed., September 1, 1922.
"Daughter born to Mr." *Leader*, February 21, 1890, evening ed. In *Abstracts
    of Items of Genealogical Interest from the Springfield, Greene County, MO
    newspapers for 1890 and 1884*. Edited by William K. Hall. St. Louis, MO:
    n.p., 1994. 42.

"Death Claims Business Man of Springfield." *Leader*, January 23, 1930, evening ed.

"Ginsburg-Karchmer." *Leader*, October 31, 1921, evening ed.

"Glaser tells club of his native land." *Leader*, November 19, 1929, evening ed.

"Jacob Rothschild Dies at Home Here After Long Illness." *Leader*, May 15, 1925, evening ed.

"Mary Wennerman." *Leader*, July 20, 1922, evening ed.

"Marx Funeral Set for Friday." *Leader*, November 22, 1928.

"Meyer E. LeBolt." *Leader*, December 27, 1933, evening ed.

"Mike Zay." *Leader*, January 11, 1921, evening ed. In *Abstracts of Items of Genealogical Interest from the Springfield, Missouri, Newspapers for 1921.* Edited by William K. Hall. St. Louis, MO: William K. Hall, 1995. 19.

"Mrs. Jake Rothschild." *Leader*, January 19, 1933, evening ed.

"Moses Levy Dies at Age of 81." *Leader*, February 20, 1928, evening ed.

"Robert E. Tinkler." *Leader*, June 11, 1921, evening ed.

"Moses Levy Dies at Age of 81." *Leader*, February 20, 1928, evening ed.

"Son born to E." *Leader*, December 30, 1889, evening ed. In *Abstracts of Items of Genealogical Interest from the Springfield, Greene County, MO newspapers for 1889.* Edited by William K. Hall. St. Louis: n.p., 1994. 235.

"Stores are Closed out of Respect to Pioneer Merchant." *Leader*, February 22, 1928, evening ed.

"Wife of Local Merchant Died This Morning." *Leader*, April 2, 1926, evening ed.

"William Arbeitman." *Leader*, March 31, 1933, evening ed.

Leader and Press

Ritchie, Mary. "English Rabbi Eyes Varied Duties." *Leader and Press*, August 20, 1972.

Leader-Democrat

"Clubs and Society." *Leader-Democrat*, March 18, 1898.

"Problems of a Church: The Jewish may take the Central Congregational." *Leader-Democrat*, January 14, 1899.

"The swellest society event." *Leader-Democrat*, September 23, 1897.

Lumber Trade Journal

"Lee Ullman." *Lumber Trade Journal*, February 1, 1911.

Men's Wear: The Retailers Newspaper

"Cohen Bros. & Co." *Men's Wear: The Retailers Newspaper*, February 5, 1908.

"New Wholesale Clothing Firm." *Men's Wear: The Retailers Newspaper*, August 7, 1907.

Missouri Weekly Patriot

"L. Ullman." Advertisement. *Missouri Weekly Patriot*, January 31, 1867. Trade Palace Advertisement. *Missouri Weekly Patriot*, April 9, 1868.

"Victor Sommers." *Missouri Weekly Patriot*, December 30, 1875: 2.

Motor World

"William Ullman." *Motor World*, June 2, 1915.

Morning News

"Last Man's Club Banquet Planned." *Morning News*, November 8, 1935.

Neosho Times

"Ulllmann [sic] and Maas." Advertisement. *Neosho Times*, February 10, 1870.

News and Leader

"Mrs. Della LeBolt." *News and Leader*, October 20, 1929, morning ed.

News-Leader

"Fannie Arbeitman." *News-Leader*, May 31, 2006.

Goodman, Ed. "New Year brings changes for Hebrew congregation." *News-Leader*, October 6, 1984.

_____. "Rabbi was children's best friend." *News-Leader*, October 16, 1983.

O'Dell, Kathleen. "Rabbi, Med Center differ on reasons behind firing." *News-Leader*, May 24, 1991.

_____. "Springfield congregation to install first female rabbi." *News-Leader*, July 30, 1992.

"A rabbi's return." *News-Leader*, May 18, 1985.

Sherwin, Rita. "Casual names-calling can hurt." *News-Leader*, October 3, 1994.

_____. Jewish Holy days' message: hope." *News-Leader*, September 20, 1993.

_____. "Many true paths head to one Truth." *News-Leader*, October 11, 1993.

Temple, Christine. "Leaving Her Mark." *News-Leader*, April 26, 2014.

Temple, Christine and Jonathan Shorman. "Faith leaders gather to advocate for human dignity." *News-Leader*, April 11, 2014.

Wicken, Tamlya. "Rabbi seeks post near home in East." *News-Leader*, September 4, 1997.

Wolff, Francie. "Historic alliance, call for diversity leads to joining NAACP." *News-Leader*, 24 January 24, 2011.

Ozarko

"Science Hall." *Ozarko*. Springfield, MO: Missouri State University, 1925. 197.

Piqua Daily Call

"Dies Suddenly." *Piqua Daily Call* [Ohio], September 17, 1905.

Republican

"Daniel H. Herman." *Republican*, February 1, 1908, morning ed. In *Abstracts of Items of Genealogical Interest from the Springfield, Greene County, MO newspapers for 1908*. Edited by William K. Hall. St. Louis, MO: n.p., 1994. 17.

"Daughter born." *Republican*, December 27, 1889, morning ed. In *Abstracts of Items of Genealogical Interest from the Springfield, Greene County, MO newspapers for 1889*. Edited by William K. Hall. St. Louis, MO: n.p., 1994. 233.

"Early Days in Springfield." *Republican*, May 23 1926, morning ed.

"Gordon-Samors." *Republican*, June 3, 1923, morning ed.

"Gus Marx." *Republican*, July 6, 1887, morning ed. In *Abstracts of Items of Genealogical Interest from the Springfield, Greene County, MO newspapers for 1883 and 1887*. Edited by William K. Hall. St. Louis, MO: n.p., 1993, 43.

"Herman-Baer." *Republican*, May 4, 1926, morning ed.

"Mrs. Charles Altschul." *Republican*, July 24, 1901, morning ed. In *Abstracts of Items of Genealogical Interest from the Springfield, Greene County, MO newspapers for 1907*. Edited by William K. Hall. St. Louis, MO: n.p., 1994. 71.

"Mrs. Hanna Marx." *Republican*, December 25, 1906: 2. In *Abstracts of Items of Genealogical Interest from the Springfield, Greene County, MO newspapers for 1906 and 1884*. Edited by William K. Hall. St. Louis, MO: William K. Hall, n.d. 124.

"Simon Rothschild." *Republican*, December 27, 1907, morning ed.

Sedalia Bazoo

"Simon Levy." *Sedalia Bazoo*, February 5, 1883.

Sedalia Democrat

Snow, Harlan B. "S.F.D. 100 Years," *Sedalia Democrat*, May 26, 1968.

Sedalia Weekly Democrat

David Levy & Bro. Advertisement. *Sedalia Weekly Democrat*, April 10, 1877.

Southwest Standard

"Rabbi Ernest I. Jacobs." *Southwest Standard*, March 17, 1950.

Springfield!

Spears-Stewart, Reta. "The Lotvens Reunion in Springfield." *Springfield!* July 1998.

Stewart, Hope V. "The Lady Is a Rabbi!" *Springfield!* 1992.

Springfield Daily Democrat

"'The American Jews' Synopsis of a Lecture by Rabbi H. Berkowitz, D.D., of Kansas City," *Springfield Daily Democrat*, March 15 1892.

Springfield Daily Leader

"Albert Silberberg Has Purchased the Entire Bankrupt Stock of Victor Sommers." *Springfield Daily Leader*, February 21, 1887.

Temple of Fashion Advertisement. *Springfield Daily Leader*, February 12, 1887.

Springfield Daily News

Mangalimam, Jessie. "City Rabbi Kaplan dies at 60." *Springfield Daily News*, October 11, 1983.

Springfield Daily Republican

"Services at Synagogue on the Jewish New Year," *Springfield Daily Republican*, September 7, 1907.

Springfield Democrat

"The little child." *Springfield Democrat*, October 27, 1893, morning ed. In *Springfield, Greene County, Missouri Newspaper Abstracts 1893-1894*. Edited by William Kearney Hall. Springfield, MO: Ozarks Genealogical Society, 1987. 72.

"Rosh Hassanah," *Springfield Democrat*, September 12, 1893.

Star Clothing House Advertisement. *Springfield Democrat*, April 20, 1868.

Springfield Express

"Died at Cleveland." Springfield Express May 5, 1882. In *Marsha Rising Abstracts*. Accessed October 26, 2015. www.warrencarmack.com/ MarshaRising/newspapers/Springfield/1882.html

Springfield Leader

Boston Store Advertisement. *Springfield Leader*, April 2, 1886.

City of Springfield vs. Albert Silberberg. *Springfield Leader*, February 1891.

The Greatest Clothing Sale Advertisement. *Springfield Leader*, October 18, 1886.

Herman the Tailor Advertisement. *Springfield Leader*. August 25, 1886.

Kamnixer, Prinz & Co. v. Rothschild. *Springfield Leader*. November 27,1890.

Kitzinger, Tuholske and Frohlichstein v. Rothschild. *Springfield Leader*, October 1, 1891.

"Married, at Carthage yesterday…" *Springfield Leader*, May 1886.

"Michael J. Weinberg vs. Moses Levy." *Springfield Leader*, October 1, 1891.

"New Company Handles Nash." *Springfield Leader*, July 31, 1927.

Opening the Campaign Advertisement. *Springfield Leader*, September 13, 1886.

"Our Healthy Climate." *Springfield Leader*, January 18, 1888.

"The Railroad. First Train Over the Ozark Mountains," *Springfield Leader*, April 22, 1870.

Schwab Clothing Co. v Rothschild. *Springfield Leader*, November 6, 1890.
"Sixteen Deaths." *Springfield Leader*, January 23, 1930.
Trade-Palace Advertisement. *Springfield Leader*, May 12, 1886.
"Twenty Five Years Ago [1885]." *Springfield Leader*, September 6, 1920.
"The Ullman family." *Springfield Leader*, September 17, 1919.
War in the Southwest! Advertisement. *Springfield Leader*, May 31, 1877.

Springfield Missouri Republican

"BANKRUPCY NO. 1214." *Springfield Missouri Republican*, June 6, 1926.
"Deaths: Jacob Wennerman." *Springfield Missouri Republican*, March 3, 1920.
"Deaths: Max Breadman." *Springfield Missouri Republican*, May 8, 1926.
"Expansion is Planned." *Springfield Missouri Republican*, April 14, 1926.
"Former Springfield Man Presented Jewish Bible During Scopes Hearing,"
Springfield Missouri Republican, July 24, 1925.
"Funeral Services." *Springfield Missouri Republican*, May 29, 1917: 8.
"In the matter of Mike Sussman." *Springfield Missouri Republican*,
    March 26, 1926.
"The Local Lodge." *Springfield Missouri Republican*, January 1, 1924.
"M. Breadman ends his life." *Springfield Missouri Republican*, May 7, 1926.
"The marriage of Miss Della Levy." *Springfield Missouri Republican*,
    September 23, 1897.
"Mrs. Simon Hirsch." *Springfield Missouri Republican*, January 6, 1901.
"Named Guardian." *Springfield Missouri Republican*, April 2, 1920.
"Pioneer is Dead." *Springfield Missouri Republican*, September 15, 1926.
"This Is the Forfeiture Contract." *Springfield Missouri Republican*,
    November 6, 1910. 26.

Springfield News & Leader

Upton, Lucile Morris. "Twelve Years Here Have Been Happy Ones for Rabbi
    Jacob Finds Peace in Springfield." *Springfield News & Leader*,
    November 28, 1954.

Springfield News-Leader

"Jewish Tradition: Book Fate Opened on New Year," *Springfield News-Leader*,
    September 17, 1909.

Springfield Republican

"Jewish Churches here Consolidate," *Springfield Republican*, June 27, 1917.
"Jacob Cohn married Minnie Longedon." *Springfield Republican*. April 3, 1896.

The Model Advertisement. *Springfield Republican*, July 17, 1898.
  "A Perfect Man," *Springfield Republican*, December 15, 1895.
"Yom Kippur Observed By Springfield Jews." *Springfield Republican*,
    October 7, 1916.

Springfield Weekly Republication
"Jewish Services." *Springfield Weekly Republication*, October 11, 1894.

Star News
"World War I vet gets the bubbly." *Star News*, February 15, *1992.*

Tampa Bay Times
Goffard, Christopher. "Keeper of Faith." *Tampa Bay Times*, April 21, 2005.

Temple Talk
Sherwin, Rita. "In Memoriam. Jake Lotven." *Temple Talk*, January 2008. OJA.

Times
"Miss Carrie Block," *Times*, January 5, 1902.

Tulsa Jewish Review
"Museum Gala to Honor Pioneer Tulsa Jewish Businessmen." *Tulsa Jewish
    Review*, August 3, 2011.

Speeches
  Lilienthal, Max. "Modern Judaism." Presented at Thanksgiving Indianap-olis,
    Indiana, 1865. Reprinted in *Max Lilienthal: American Rabbi: Life and
    Writings*. Edited by David Philpson. New York: Bloch, 1915. 444-453.
  Evans, Hiram W. "The Attitude of the Knights of the Ku Klux Toward the Jew,"
    in *Papers Read at the Meeting of Grand Dragons Knights of the Ku Klux Klan
    At their First Annual Meeting held at Asheville, North Carolina, July 1923*, E.
    F. Randolph, 1923, pp. 117-122.